**XAVIERA HAS CONSUMMATED
HER MASTERPIECE—
AS SHE PROVES THAT
PRACTICE HAS MADE PERFECT!**

There is only one Xaviera Hollander, and this is the book that brings her entire erotic career to a rousing and unrivaled climax.

Your joy of sex will rise to its ultimate volcanic peak as she shows you surefire ways to liberate both your imagination and your body from any ignorance or inhibitions holding you back from the tops in pleasure and performance.

Why, she even shows you the missionary position!

Which gives you some idea of how far our Happy Hooker has gone to make sure she provides what is just right for you. . .

XAVIERA'S SUPERSEX

SIGNET Books You'll Enjoy

If you wish to order these titles,
please see the coupon in
the back of this book.

XAVIERA'S SUPERSEX

Her Personal Techniques for Total Lovemaking

by
Xaviera Hollander

A SIGNET BOOK

NEW AMERICAN LIBRARY

TIMES MIRROR

A BERNARD GEIS ASSOCIATES BOOK

Originally appeared as an oversized illustrated
Signet special edition.

SIGNET, SIGNET CLASSICS, MENTOR, PLUME and
MERIDIAN BOOKS are published by
The New American Library, Inc., 1301 Avenue of the Americas,
New York, New York 10019.

First Signet Printing, December, 1978

1 2 3 4 5 6 7 8 9

Printed in the United States of America

Contents

Introduction

In all my other books, from *The Happy Hooker* to *Xaviera on the Best Part of a Man,* I've concentrated on telling you my sexual adventures. But in my new book, *Xaviera's Supersex,* I've decided to detail how you can embark on great sexual adventures of your own. You'll get even more out of *Supersex* than you did from my other books. And with the new goodies you'll discover in these pages, you'll have more delights to share with your partner in bed.

These are my "official" lessons in love. I'm going to concentrate not so much on what I've done as on what I've *learned* from what I've done. I'll *tell* you, point by point, how you can be better in bed than you ever thought possible. If you came to me in person for a course in supersexmanship, I couldn't show you in the flesh more clearly than this.

Ready for lesson one? Let's begin!

Xaviera

1. Foreplay Is Never Having to Say "Are You Ready?"

Germaine Greer said: "Every man should be fucked in the ass so he knows what it feels like to be penetrated."

The lady has a point. Different men will, of course, react differently to that statement. While most men have homosexual yearnings, few men really want a homosexual partner in their beds. But in sex as in any other relationship in life, success depends on seeing things from the other person's point of view. One thing is for sure: men would have to learn that penetration without preparation is no way to make 'em beg for more.

Most men are self-conscious, and therefore self-centered, about foreplay. A typical example of what goes wrong with so much of our lovemaking is the comment by an earnest husband to his marriage counselor: "I guess my foreplay needs more work."

Too many people emphasize the fore instead of the play, so that instead of an erotic game that's pleasing to both participants in its own right, it becomes a dutiful preliminary to something More Important. This is one of the drawbacks of the sexual revolution. Nowadays, when two people start something, they know that they're free to end up in bed and finish it. In the old days, couples who didn't dare "go all the way" were able to enjoy some really great foreplay, necking and petting up to the point of what used to be called "the limit." There was nothing More Important than what they were doing to each other at any given moment. They knew that social mores prevented them from actually having intercourse, so they got a lot more kicks out of their tantalizing foreplay.

No part of the love act is less important than the whole; a kiss can be just as meaningful as actual penetration. Keep this in mind and you'll be a better lover, because foreplay *never* begins in the bed. It begins in the head. Ideally, foreplay (formerly known as seduction) is the art of keeping your lover in a perpetual state of erotic awareness; it can be just a look that zeroes in on another human being and says: "You turn me on." And *that* is what will turn your *partner* on too.

The purpose of foreplay is to create sexual titillation, and titillation is best served by surprise. A man's chief enemy in foreplay is predictability. He sticks to a tried-and-true lovemaking pattern because it seemed to work on the last four women. He forgets that each woman is an individual. Don't forget what I said about the other person's point of view. Men classify themselves as "tit men," "ass men," or "leg men," but they often forget that women themselves, on the receiving end, have their own preferences. The most sensitive part of a woman varies from individual to individual, and must be taken into consideration. What happens when he prefers the low road and she prefers the high road? I say the woman's preferences should determine the course. Then, when she's in a delicious frenzy, she'll love a few detours to her nether regions.

This is not to say that women don't have foreplay faults, too. A woman's biggest mistake is false innocence: she's afraid to let her sexual expertise show for fear that her lover will think she's been around too much. Though she wants to fondle his penis and perhaps suck it, she'll wait until he guides her hand and asks her to "do" him. If she does something really daring, she's afraid that he might, like the husband in *Diary of a Mad Housewife*, say: "Where the hell did you learn *that*?" That happens maybe once in a hundred cases. The other ninety-nine times, the man will be delirious with joy. Play the odds.

Behold the Foreplay Freak

The man I call a Foreplay Freak always starts at the top and works down. The scenario is as rigid as an Amtrak timetable, and just as Philadelphia comes before Washington, so breasts must precede clitoris. He would never dream of proceeding in any other way. He is also hung up on "equal time." He gives each breast exactly the same treatment, plays with each nipple before kissing it, and then trails his free hand down his girl's belly to stroke her clitoris—because everybody knows that this is the right order in which to proceed. Gone is the delicious suspense of wondering what the next move is to be, and the awakening and arousal that each new unexpected touch stirs into being.

He wishes he could think of something to do

with his other hand. Then, when inspiration strikes him at last, he discovers he can't move. He's been propped up on his elbows so he could loom over her properly, and his arm has gone to sleep and become numb. Sometimes it's caught under her shoulders, so he'll attempt to reach under and around her far enough to touch her other breast, but this creates an even worse problem in maneuverability.

His woman is not really warmed up yet, but he is now stroking her clitoris, so . . . She knows that intercourse is supposed to come a few minutes after this, and she decides to fake a passion she doesn't really feel so that he won't think she's frigid—and thus get the whole thing over with. After all, he's touched bottom now, and there's no place to go but *in*.

She doesn't even have to go to bed to get this kind of routine. She could get the same program watching television: it's called *Upstairs, Downstairs.*

There Are No Erroneous Zones

So much for the conventional approach to foreplay. Exciting sex is, by definition, unconventional—meaning that the best things you can do are those that would shock *somebody* out there.

Now, try these surprise turn-ons. They work on both sexes and need not be done in any order—which is why I'm shuttling back and forth between the sexes. Foreplay is a game for two, to be played in no sequence and to be initiated by either the man or the woman, as the mood and the occasion suggest.

- Eyelashes. Flick them over lips, nipples, or the underside of the penis tip. Go slowly at first, then increase your blinking speed. The popular name for this technique is "the butterfly," which is probably why too many men ignore it. Eyelashes are thought of as feminine, but men's lashes are often thicker and more bristly, so they make better and sexier brushes, right? Right!

- Licking. Take a shower together and then lick the water off of each other. You'll never use a towel again. (At this point you're probably wondering how you can lick a body dry when you *wet* a stamp by licking it. The answer is that you can't. It's just that it's fun trying.)

- Silk scarves. Pull them between your lover's thighs. Start just above the knees and work your way up to the crotch. When the scarf is wet, you'll know it's time to stop and get on to other things. (Check the label first to make sure it doesn't say "dry clean only.")

- Spines. To rid yourself of the upstairs-downstairs habit, start in the middle. Nibble gently, flicking your tongue as you go, first in one direction, then in the other. The most sensitive cluster of nerves is at the base of the spine, or coccyx, just above the buttocks. Take big, gentle bites of the cheeks, french kiss the flesh, suck it into your mouth, then lick the crease where the thighs begin. Talk about spine-tingling excitement!

• And while you're down there . . . Since both men and women wear their hair much longer than they used to, this can be put to good use, too. Men with very long hair can trail it between a woman's legs, up and down her crotch. Women with long hair can do something even better: wrap it around their lover's penis, pulling snugly to make a silken vise for him. Tighten and release, a sort of "squeeze technique." The pleasure is the same, but using long, silky hair instead of fingers is more romantic—and certainly a lot more novel!

• Nails. Not for women only, as Barbara Walters would say. A man can discover things he's never really noticed before if he uses his nails properly. Men aren't the only ones who have "back hair"; most women have a downy, colorless growth in the small of the back and on the buttocks. It's so faint that men aren't usually aware of it, especially if they caress this area with hefty squeezes. A man should pull his woman's buttocks taut and run his nails gently across her firm, tightened flesh, savoring her baby-fine hairs. She can do the same thing to his buttocks, and also to his shoulders if he's at all hairy there.

• Navels. An "inner"-type navel can be tongued; an "outer" can be sucked. A really deep inner can be a little cup. Pour honey in it and then sip on the nectar like the birds and the bees your parents once told you about.

• Pelvic nerves. These are located at the juncture where thigh meets torso, extending up to the knobs of the pelvic bones. Hitting the right place with either tongue or finger, or one of each, produces a reaction like that of an electric shock. The body jerks and begins to arch like a cartwheel as the delicious hot-cold feeling increases.

Breasts—Not Up for Grabs

Women can get "hit where it hurts," too. Some women's breasts are so sensitive that merely going without a bra can make them ache. Men would have much more success with breasts if they'd bear in mind that they're as sensitive as their own testicles.

Men classify women according to the size of their breasts, then handle them the way they think each size deserves. A woman with big breasts often gets mauled and kneaded like bread dough because men can't resist her generous endowment. They don't think she minds the roughness because they equate size with sturdiness. Consequently—and this is one of the big ironies of sex—the bosomy woman sometimes gets more torture than pleasure out of her breasts.

Men go easier on small breasts, sometimes out of lack of interest but more often out of instinctive gentleness with little things. So it's the woman with the lemon-sized breasts who gets the kind of treatment from a lover that every woman wants. Unfair, I say, speaking as one of the more generously endowed.

Points About Points

• One of the best ways to warm up a small- or medium-breasted woman is to take the whole breast into your mouth. A man who can perfect a rhythmic swallowing motion and pinch the nipples in the back of his throat will drive a lucky woman wild.

• A little sucking goes a long way—and a lot can be a bore. A nipple will soon grow numb if a man clamps his mouth over it and never lets up. A lick and a promise is much better, along with a gentle nibble. The first rule is: *Let the air get to it*. Lift the mouth completely away from the breast and stretch your tongue out to meet her nipple.

• Next to the nipple, most of a woman's sensations of touch are in the areola, popularly known as the "pink part," though it's sometimes more tan in brunettes and older women; in black and Indian women it's a luscious chocolate brown. Some women have a naturally swollen areola, so that it looks like a walnut even when she's not excited. Others have a flat areola that wrinkles up into a knot under stimulation, and though I can't absolutely guarantee this, it seems to me that wrinkly areolas have more feeling.

Lick around the rim of the areola, circling slowly as you come closer to the nipple itself. Flick the nipple with your tongue, then return to the now wrinkled areola until nipple and areola are one long knotty tongue flicking back at you. (This one makes me *very* hot.)

• How to blow a girl . . . Yes, it *can* be done above the waist! I can't emphasize strongly enough how easily excited nipples are. The least little thing will make them hard; I once had a bra with a poorly stitched lining, and the slight lumpy fold in the seam kept hitting my nipple and driving me crazy all day long. I loved it, I loved it.

Blow on your woman's nipples. Have some wine at the bedside and pour a few drops directly on the nipples, then blow dry. The combination of icy wine and warm breath will make her high, in the nicest possible way.

• Although there's little erotic sensation between the breasts, the term "cleavage" is such a suggestive word that the area can take on some psychological feeling. Take a breast in each hand, cup it gently, then squeeze them together to form a deep sexy cleavage. Place your thumbs on each nipple while you lick up and down the crease. Massage the nipples with your thumbs, brushing them lightly back and forth. Breathe heavily to make passionate sounds and to add the sensation of your warm breath.

• Many men have mustaches and beards that can be put to good use. Swish bristly facial hair over her nipples. It could spell a permanent end to the clean-shaven look.

• An area of the breast all too often ignored is the underside crease. Applying your tongue to this crease is especially effective because it's especially unexpected.

• Women with large or pendulous breasts may enjoy having them gently jiggled. The feeling of weightiness is quite a turn-on—to both partners. The areolas of pendulous breasts are very sensitive, and usually large, sometimes as big as silver dollars. A man should sit up in bed, leaning back against the headboard, while his woman sits between his legs with her back to him. He reaches around and cups her breasts with his hands. He should not let his tongue or penis go to waste at this moment: tongue her ear and press your penis into her back, while whispering a fantasy scenario. Pretend that you are two strangers on a crowded bus, practicing *frottage* (rubbing up against people in crowds). Tell her why you would pick her out of all the other women on the bus, then make her tell you the sensations your nudging penis is giving her.

• The look-no-hands massage can add a healthy and natural game of foreplay to the sexual repertoire. But first let's start with more familiar massage techniques. Offering to ease someone's aching muscles is an innocent, even neighborly thing to do, and helps to get loveplay off to a relaxed start.

Thanks to massages, either party can be the doer or the do-ee—the first rule of good foreplay, remember—without self-consciousness. A massage is an especially good way to get a man on his back without making him feel passive.

Without a narrow, professional masseur's table, however, most massaging has to be done in a wide, bouncy bed, which means that in order to reach your "subject," you have to crawl all over him or her. Is that bad? However, if you're serious about the massage, you can do a better job on the floor, especially if there's a nice deep-pile rug. If not, spread a couple of blankets on the floor.

Now we come to the no-hands technique, a sensitive, delicately thrilling bit of business for those who are handy with their breasts. A woman can give nipple rubdowns that stimulate both herself and her lover. Have your man lie first on his stomach. Straddle his shoulders, a knee on the outside of each, your legs spread nice and wide. Lean down and trail your breasts back and forth over his head, then his neck. Bend over in a jackknife position, and taking your breast in your hand, guide your nipple around his ear. Then move to the other breast and the other ear. As you work your way down his back with breasts in hand, press them firmly against his ribs where the "tickle spots" are located.

When you've traveled far enough down his back so that your spread legs are directly over his buttocks, ease down gently and rub your pubic hair across his rump. If you have a generous bush, the feel of the now-wet hairs trailing over his buttocks will drive him wild. Press down harder and wriggle quickly, then let up. Do this down the back of his thighs; when your breasts are directly above his buttocks, spread his cheeks with your hands and dip first one breast, then the other, between them. Trail the nipples up and down his anal crevice and aim one into his rim. If you lubricate the nipple, you can insert it a tiny bit into his anus. When you do this, he should squeeze his sphincter muscle around it.

Continue trailing your nipples down his legs, concentrating on the backs of his knees. Finally, kneel on the floor at the bottom of the bed and tickle the back of his feet with your nipples, pushing them between his toes.

Now turn him over on his back and start the whole process again. The aroma of his body will have clung to your breasts and will excite him as you trail them over his face. Dip your breasts into the hollows of his neck—an erogenous zone for men, too, and one that too many women ignore. When your breasts are over his chest, gently squeeze his nipples until you have pulled them up into tiny breasts, then match yours to his. Stocky men often have enough flesh on their chests to form actual breasts. This can be a powerful stimulus to the normal bisexuality found in everyone.

Slip down to his stomach and insert a nipple into his navel. By now you're straddling his crotch, so tease his penis with your vagina. Back up to it so that it's lying up against your buttocks. Bend forward slowly, letting it slide down between and then under your legs. Trail it through your crotch, lifting your body up so that it no more than dabs the inner lips of your vagina. When it emerges and slaps up against your belly, push against it gently, taking care not to force it too firmly against its natural angle. Nudge it and let it rest against your belly while you savor its throbs, then do some bumps and grinds against it.

You probably think you're ready for the climax now. You're probably right, but this is only the beginning of my catalog of tricks. It's now time to turn the merely erotic into the totally exotic.

2. Fiveplay, Sixplay, and Sevenplay

Extended foreplay is something that everyone wants, but most people are reluctant to "fool around" too long. Men fear the loss of erection—and even more than that, the loss of face that would accompany it. Women worry that making a man wait too long will cause him actual physical pain—known as "blue balls" back in the days when necking sessions went on for hours with no release in sight.

There's a lot to be said for getting down to business—the strike-while-the-iron-is-hot school of thought. There's even something to be said for the quickie, impure and simple, short and sweet—and I'll say it in a later chapter. But every once in a while, it's good to really stretch things out and "make a night of it" by driving each other almost but not quite crazy with frustration. "Unendurable pleasure indefinitely prolonged" is not a bad way to pass the time of night.

Pretend you're both a couple of horny high-school virgins back in the days before the pill as you try some of these delicious torments.

When Did You Last Have a Knee Ride?

The famous knee ride has long been a lesbian practice, but it's a turn-on for any couple who can, between them, provide one clitoris and one knee.

The pressure of a woman's moist crotch pressing and sliding on his thigh and knee can be thrilling to a man. One man I know said this practice makes up for his small penis. "I pretend my thigh is the biggest cock in the world, and my knee the biggest head. My woman goes wild mounting it, and she gets so hot that she squirms her vagina down on my kneecap as if she's really trying to insert it. I get off on it too, because she's so turned on that my fantasy seems almost real."

Another friend of mine gives a very different account of this practice. "Every guy secretly wants a woman who is all things to all men. When my woman rides my knee, it's as if she were a little girl playing 'ride a cock-horse to Banbury Cross' on her daddy's lap, as well as a big girl who's terrific in bed with her sugar daddy."

Knee-riding is a big help for the woman who has trouble reaching orgasm. Many women climax fairly soon after they start to hump anything because it reminds them, consciously or unconsciously, of the first form of masturbation they indulged in when they were very young and rode a pillow or wadded a blanket. The childhood sexual release that this kind of activity recalls can help a woman throw off her inhibitions and achieve a spontaneous orgasm.

A woman's climaxing during a knee ride will thrill most men. Men are fascinated by the idea of "female ejaculation." This is supposedly a myth, but we all know that women get very wet when they come, and if a man wants, he can lick his thigh to taste it. I know several men who love to do this.

The Penis as Vibrator

We are living in an era in which the vibrator is often used as a penis substitute that we almost forget what the penis can do single-handed, so to speak. All that's lacking is the buzz, and if a woman must have her buzz—would you believe, some women can't function too well without it?— she can always leave his electric shaver buzzing away nearby while she enjoys a real-live penis massage.

A hard penis is one up on a vibrator—it's sexy, soft and hard at the same time, and it throbs. The underside of the penis contains a big artery; when the shaft is pressed firmly against a woman's skin, she can feel the pulsations like a heartbeat. That's when the drums start beating in the jungle!

The penile massage can start at either end and work up or down accordingly. One of the most exciting things a man can do for a woman is start with her head and give her a hard cock *in her hair*. Here's how.

Kneel over her face with your balls resting on her mouth so that she can lick and kiss them while you part her hair with your penis. Push forward and lift portions of her hair, as a hairdresser does with a comb to separate the hair into sections for setting. Then nudge her around the ears with it; finally, steer into the thickest part of her hair and tangle your penis in it. If her hair is still warm from a dryer, it might feel so good that you'll come—in which case she'll have a built-in protein conditioner. Warren Beatty in *Shampoo* never did it so good! And it's a good excuse to take a shower together, too.

Light, teasing thrusts to the ears, armpits, the bend of the elbow, and the wrists make a woman feel completely loved because your penis is interested in all of her, not just her genitals. A penile "kiss" on her nipples can be especially arousing if you push the tip of your penis against the tip of her nipple, and then rub the frenulum (the membrane fold underneath the penis where the glans and foreskin come together) back and forth over her areola, savoring the roughness of her nubby circles. Remember, the more lubrication you use on both your penis and her nipples, the more sensations can be felt. Dryness will numb both areas and even make this loveplay painful. A fun lubricant is whipped cream from an aerosol can (not cold, please) or any one of the flavored love jellies that you can eat off later.

Gently prod her navel, her pelvic nerves, the knobs of her pelvic bones, the puff of pubic hair at the bottom of her stomach, the backs of her knees, the small of her back, the area between her shoulderblades. Then, as a finale, press your hard penis against the arteries in her neck. By now they should be as hard and throbbing as the artery in

your penis. Let them throb together, two hearts
beating as one.

The Foot, Le Pied, Der Fuss—Mit Toes, Too

The foot is the western world's most ignored
tertiary sex organ. The Orientals, Persians, and
Indians have known for centuries—and painted
pictures to demonstrate—that feet, and the big toe
in particular, are marvelous assistant penises.
That's how one emperor could satisfy a harem full
of wives and concubines. Look, Ma, no hands.

Feet have a bad reputation because they are the
most utilitarian parts of our bodies. Partly for this
reason, but mostly because of a lack of imagination, the foot is not commonly thought of as a sex
organ.

But the foot as sex symbol is something else.
The bare foot is a symbol of guilt-free, primitive
peoples, and today, if a woman kicks off her shoes
or goes barefoot, it's a hint that she's sexually un-
hung-up. The erotic symbolism of the dainty female foot is well-known, from stories of ancient
Chinese foot-binding to the fairy tale of Cin-
derella. The small foot also looks great in high
heels, a turn-on for men because they look . . .
well, whorish. Though a psychoanalyst I know
told me they looked phallic. But to a psychoanalyst, doesn't everything?

Obviously, we are confused about feet. The way
to end this confusion is to enjoy the things your
feet can do in bed, when you have no intention of
going anywhere, by foot or otherwise. Besides, the

man who uses his foot will have a dick that can stay and play another day.

• Toe job (hers). The woman should lubricate between her big and second toes, which are acting as substitute thumb and forefinger, so that he can ease his penis in and out of the space.

• Toe job (his). He lubricates his big toe and inserts it (making sure the nail is clipped short) into the vagina. The woman can take it in the missionary position, or on her hands and knees, facing the bottom of the bed while the man sits up against the headboard. She can also stand on the floor at the bottom of the bed, legs spread and body bent forward.

• Foot job (hers). She wiggles all ten lubricated toes up and down the penile shaft, or grips the penis at its base with big and second toe, holding it firmly while she squeezes the tip with the big and second toes of her other foot.

• Foot job (his). He can tickle her—in the most ticklish zone of all—with the toes of one or both feet. One way is by pressing his big toe against her clitoris and dabbing lightly, almost not touching it at all. He can try another variation by lying on his back with his feet over the edge of the mattress while she spreads her legs and lowers herself against the pad of his toe. Or both partners can lie at opposite ends of the bed while he massages her entire crotch with his foot.

• Bugger your toe. An English game. Anyone

can play provided the partners can bring one big toe and one anus to the sport. One partner inserts his or her big toe into the other's anal rim and moves it gently up and down. The receiving party should half-sit, half-stand at the bottom of the bed, thighs on the mattress, and backside upturned.

Would You Believe—Even Moreplay?

Now we come to that ultimate crazy-maker, what girls used to call "doing everything but" and boys used to call "cock-teasing." But as much as they all complained about it, they loved every minute of it because it included some of the most sensual acts a man and a woman can perform together. Twenty years ago, before coed dorms, the pill, and a less puritanical attitude toward sex made their appearance, the scene of the "crime" was usually the back seat of a car or a blanket in a secluded outdoors spot. The latter was actually the best place, because things can get pretty messy. Make sure you have lots of towels handy and, ideally, a bathroom.

• The thigh squeeze. The woman should use an artificial lubricant between her thighs—if she needs one. Usually she won't; a happy vagina will seep its own juices onto the upper thighs to make them nice and slippery.

A thigh squeeze can be done in any number of positions, but the most pleasing position for both partners is with the woman on her back and the man above. She should keep her thighs pressed tightly together and place a thick towel under them. The man lies on top of the woman with his legs spread out around hers. Balanced on his elbows, he does push-ups, thrusting his penis up and down in the satiny vise of his partner's inner thighs—one of the pleasanter forms of morning exercise.

There's an agony involved in this ecstasy: the penis should not touch the vulva at all. This was an ironclad rule in the days when girls were terrified of getting pregnant if a boy even got near her. It's still a good rule if you want to experience Xaviera's Moreplay in the *right* way. A vital element in good sex is a vivid imagination; a good practice in achieving a sexual third dimension of the mind is for both partners to convince themselves that the woman's slick, clasping thighs are really a vagina.

A thigh squeeze can also be performed in side positions, either with the couple facing each other or with the woman lying with her back to the man. My favorite position, though, is standing up with my lover behind me. In this way a woman can exercise her imagination and get off on a little harmless bisexuality at the same time. As he slides his penis through her tightly closed thighs, she'll see it emerge at the front of her body. When it's all the way through, she can take it in her fingers and make jerking off movements around its tip as she pretends that it's hers. (Go ahead and be a man for a few minutes—it's fun!) Which reminds me of Boris, a delightful Russian lover I had who tried to teach me a limited Russian vocabulary. "*Pizduh*," he explained, "is what I have that you

haven't got, but what I would gladly give to you—
only you must give it back."

• The breast squeeze. The woman lies on her
back and pushes her breasts together while her
lover kneels over her chest. His penis should be
well lubricated with an artificial substance.

While he's pushing his penis in and out of her
cleavage, she uses her thumbs to rub her own
nipples. Men get a great thrill from seeing a
woman indulge in any kind of auto-eroticism
while they make love to her. It's her way of saying: "What you're doing to me feels so good that I
have to do something to me, too." Most men think
only of turning a woman on to *them*. But it's really a greater accomplishment, and a more sophisticated way of lovemaking, to turn a woman on to
herself. Then you have a great deal in common—
you're both nuts about *her*.

The breast squeeze can be combined with fellatio if a woman places several plump pillows under
her head so that her mouth is on a line with his
penis as it emerges from her cleavage. Then she
can bob her head forward and take his penis head
into her mouth. If he knows what's good for
him—and for her—he won't break his rhythm; it's
more sensual for both parties if she flicks her
tongue over his coronal rim, gives the head a
quick suck, and then lets him take it away from
her with his back pull. This way, both partners
are "cock-teased" equally, sometimes almost beyond control.

If he comes during this game, the surprise of it
all can be oddly thrilling as he spurts forth in all
directions. Save the real blow-job for actual oral

sex and take his "surprise" on but not in your mouth, or wherever it comes. Not every woman will feel it's a turn-on, but how do you know until you've tried? You might be surprised in more ways then one.

• The cheek squeeze. The idea is not to penetrate, but to slip and slide. Therefore, the woman should not lie flat on her stomach, but on her side in a fetal position so that her buttocks form a sickle curve that the penis can follow. The woman can also kneel beside the bed, resting on her elbows as her man straddles her buttocks and moves in a squatting motion, up and down, with his penis pointed down toward the floor. Both the penis and the inside of the buttocks should be generously lubricated; as he pushes his penis up and down between her buttocks, she should grip as tightly as possible against its girth, and flex her cheek muscles in a rhythm. If she flexes vigorously enough, certain muscles will be sore the next morning—it's the same muscular stiffness that results from horseback riding, and if she's an equestrienne, she should be well equipped to perfor the cheek squeeze.

• The armpit squeeze. This technique takes a lot of womanpower—with your shoulder to the wheel if not your nose to the grindstone.

It's best for the woman to kneel, with her lover standing behind her. This way, she can rock vigorously to and fro without colliding face-on with his pelvic bones. His penis, which is tucked under her arm, is the only thing that should come between them now. He should protect his balls by cupping them in his hands and holding them back out of her way. She may either piston her arm as she would if she were running very fast, or else she may rock her entire torso to and fro in a kind of jig-time kowtow.

The woman should be sure to wash off her deodorant first, else she may give him a rash. And you know where.

• On but not in. Once again, penetration is not fair, as the name of this game implies.

The woman should lie down on her back with lots of pillows under her hips so that her lover can kneel between her legs and slide his penis up and down between her vaginal lips.

Alternatively, she can remove the pillows and lie flat on her back with her thighs clamped together. Her man straddles her, and positioning himself as for push-ups, with his cock pointed straight down, he pushes it down between her vaginal lips. A few up-and-down rubs, and she is almost certain to climax, because this technique exerts more pressure on the clitoris than actual intercourse.

Any intercourse position can be used for this technique. The woman can kneel in the puppy-dog position, with her lover kneeling behind her, where he can bisect her from the rear. Each time his penis tip emerges front-side, she can greet it with a squeeze of her hand like a friendly politician.

• Clitoral friction. A woman *could* get pregnant this way, so she should make sure she is protected. The man simply keeps his penis going in a rhythmic circular motion at the top of the woman's vulva, where the clitoris is located. When he shoots, he aims his ejaculations directly at the clitoris.

Any woman will thrill to the feeling of a sharp, intense spurt on her clitoris at this range. It's best described as a warm, syrupy trickle, and there's *nothing* quite like it, believe me. I guess it's the way a ball of ice cream would feel when the hot fudge sauce oozes over it. Men who used to win the "circle-jerk" contest in their boyhood should try this technique; they may have the jetting power to give a girl the clitoral sensations she needs for orgasm.

• Balling Jack. Some women would rather have a man who's endowed with large testicles than one with a large penis—a situation known as "all potatoes and no meat." These women claim that the feel of a man's testicles rubbing against the anal area during intercourse is the most important aid to orgasm.

A man's testicles alone can bring a woman to orgasm. Using the missionary position, the woman should spread her legs very wide and wrap them high up around her lover's back. She reaches under him and gathers his balls gently in both her hands, then nestles them snugly between her vaginal lips. Then, with her man's stiff penis lying on her belly, she moves as she would if he were actually inside her. A man with very hairy balls can tickle a woman into a climax, although it's more likely she'll be turned on by the warmth and weight of his testicles, which provide a "crowded" feeling between her legs and against her clitoris—

just like the blanket she might have humped when she was a child.

Well, maybe in addition to all this foreplay, fiveplay, sixplay, and sevenplay, there's somebody out there who knows something about eightplay. If so, I don't want to hear about it. There's plenty here to keep you occupied in a month of rainy Sundays. As for me, I'm more than ready by this time for a penetrating performance. How about you?

3. Fun-damentals; or Belly-to-Belly Basics

Good lovemaking is like good dancing: there's nothing to it as long as you start with the basics and don't try to imitate Fred Astaire right off the bat, doing classy jetés from chair to chair and finishing up on the wall. I certainly don't mean to discourage imaginative experimentation—in fact, in a later chapter I'm going to show you how to use your imagination as you've never used it before. I simply mean that you have to master the basic steps before you try Last Tango in Paris. Otherwise, it may indeed be your last tango—at least, with your present partner.

Face Your Partner

Have you heard the Hindu version of the familiar joke about the sex book? Hari had finally finished writing the *Kama Sutra* after many years of research, interviews, and personal experimentation, and had amassed a repertoire of 3,542 different positions. He showed the manuscript to his friend Krishna and asked him what he thought of it.

Krishna read the manuscript carefully, then frowned and asked, "What about the one where the girl lies down on her back and spreads her legs while the guy lies between them?"

Hari snapped his fingers. "Oh, I remember now! That's the one Lady Jane showed me."

The missionary position has been criticized lately by some militant feminists, who claim that it symbolizes male dominance, overlooking the fact that this position can give the female the greatest clitoral stimulation. So who cares who's on top? While I don't like the chauvinist who compulsively insists upon it all of the time, I believe it's the most logical and most comfortable position for couples making love together for the first time, and certainly for virgins of both sexes.

This position is also more emotionally satisfying. It permits all five senses to be exercised at once, with a minimum of effort and in the most romantic way. You can taste each other's tongues, hear the softest whisper, see into each other's eyes, smell each other's skin and hair, and embrace naturally without straining.

This is the one position you don't really have to get into—it just happens naturally. A woman who has been kissed and caressed until she's nearly wild *must* open her legs because her vagina is so swollen she can't bear to keep them closed. She'll naturally raise her leg and drape it over her man's hip. When she does this, he just as naturally falls between her thighs. They're now in position without thinking about it or breaking the rhythm of their lovemaking.

The First Step

Inserting a stiff penis into a wet and ready vagina is so easy that it's sometimes too easy. Men like to do what they call "ramming it home," and when the path is as well lubricated as it should be, that's exactly what can happen. Any actor can tell you that the most effective entrance is made when you pause at the threshold, wait for a beat, and then move on in. It's that brief pause that lets them size you up, applaud if you're a star, and hang out the welcome mat. Sliding in on a banana peel is strictly for laughs.

No matter how eager a woman is to be filled up, the shock of a sudden deep thrust deprives her of the pleasure of savoring a slow, steady penetration. Especially on her virgin night, or when she's with a new lover, a woman wants to be able to remember the moment of penetration, and she can't very well do that if it's faster than the speed of light.

The official moment of penetration occurs when she feels the fanned-out ridge of the penis head stretch open the mouth of her vaginal opening. It's a nudging sensation that suddenly makes her feel wide open. This is the moment to pause so that she can put her mind as well as her body into it.

Division of Lay-bor

Too many men take all the work upon themselves, never realizing that a woman, left to her own devices, will sail right up the pole like a flag. The man-on-top position need not result in a passive woman underneath—far from it. The position is ideal for the man to enjoy the dominance he needs for his ego, yet permits a woman to do at least half of the work, if not more.

Let your woman push *up* on your penis and wriggle it into herself. This is especially good if she's a virgin, because it relieves her fear of pain by letting her regulate the amount she feels she's capable of absorbing at one time. It also permits her to time the pauses she needs to regather her courage.

With a woman you're sleeping with for the first time, the odds are just about astronomical, of course, that she *won't* be a virgin. But here, again, letting her take some of the initiative in the missionary position is psychologically advantageous. Afterward, she won't feel as if she's been stuck, pronged, poked, and left behind in the shuffle, as women sometimes feel with new lovers who take them too fast and furiously. After all, technically speaking, if you let her meet you halfway, you can rightly say that intercourse is indeed a form of introduction, and she can truly say, "Pleased to have met you."

Best of all, letting a woman call some of the moves gives you a chance to discover her sexual rhythms, movements, and general all-around internal shape and size, and thus to prepare to accommodate and match them to yours. If she has a small vagina, you'll find out before she screams bloody murder; if she's on the large side, you can position yourself accordingly before you fall out of her. (I'll tell you how later.)

It's Not the Man, It's the Motion

One of women's chief complaints is: "I wish men would *wiggle* more!"

Despite the recent discovery of the importance of the clitoris and the discrediting of Sigmund Freud's theory that all female sensations are in the vagina, many men still believe in the plug-and-socket theory. They think that the vagina is full of exposed nerves, like a broken tooth, and that a woman goes crazy the minute *anything* enters her. What the vagina *is* full of are rolling, ridgelike wrinkles that make a man go crazy when his penis is rubbing back and forth against them, like a piece of oversexed laundry getting a rub-a-dub on the washboard.

Simply receiving a man's thrusts will not bring a woman to climax. No matter how long he can keep up this simple-minded approach, his woman is more likely to get sore—in more ways than one—than to get off. What does bring her to climax is having a nice stiff penis in there, *plus* weight, pressure, and friction on her entire genital area (especially that lively little she-devil, the clitoris), as well as on her thighs and stomach.

It's the *way* a man presses down on her, puts his weight on her, and rubs her with his body that makes her have an orgasm, and a man can't do these things if he positions himself on his knees and elbows and simply thrusts and pulls. Many men, out of a mistaken sense of chivalry, take care not to lie on top of a woman too heavily and mash her down. They think they're supposed to give her room to move freely, but often they give her too much room—so much sometimes that she might as well be making it with a vibrator. I've always loved the feeling of a male belly rotating against mine, a hairy male chest against my breasts, and *then* when he plugs in, the lights flash and the bells ring for the big jackpot.

Roll with the Punches

To start with, put your legs flat and lift yourself on your elbows so that your pelvic area is crushed against hers and yet your chest isn't crashing against hers. Push your penis all the way into her vagina as far as it will go, gently at first and then firmly; then move your hips in rhythmic circular motion.

She will quickly follow suit and arch the small of her back until her clitoris is up against your crotch. As you move together, the clitoris will receive a maximum of friction from your pubic bone, as well as all the tickling it could ask for from your pubic hair.

To create even more mutual pelvic pressure, the woman can rest her legs flat on the bed. When both partners keep their legs flat, their bodies are in the utmost convex position, with the greatest degree of upcurve being in their pelvic regions.

To take a leaf from my introductory remarks, it's like dancing—wriggling hips, bumps and grinds, and moving rhythmically against each other while pressed crotch-to-crotch. The rumba, the samba, and the cha-cha got their start on a mattress, with a mistress. Somewhere along the line the partners married and became respectable, but the memory of their lovemaking was carried over vertically to the dance floor. At least, that's the Xaviera version of dance history. Anybody got a better one?

Bedroom Boo-Boos—Men

I'm not trying to deny you men your own style. I simply want to tell you how you can help a woman come first. After she climaxes, you can do all the things you like to do, the way you like to do them. The reason many women can't have an orgasm is that they try to emulate a man's lovemaking or are too quick to accommodate men in the following practices—all strictly no-nos:

• Don't grip her legs too tightly. In fact, don't grip at all until she has come. Too many men insist that a woman lie with her knees bent so that they can grip her thighs in the crook of their elbows. I know it's nice to savour armfuls of succulent thighs, but it moves your woman out of the most advantageous position for her. She's not going anywhere, remember, but she'll *want* to get up and leave if you make her feel like a prisoner in the town stocks.

• Don't hold on for dear life to her cheeks. Her buttocks aren't going anywhere, either, but men love to reach under and scoop them up anyway. Some men pinch, and others hold on so tightly that she can't make full undulatory motions. Remember, the rule is: Let *her* rip.

• Don't stand on her head. It's easy to spot a selfish man; the moment he climbs in bed he orders, "Put 'em up!" Some want the girl's legs straight up in the air; others demand that she drape her feet over their shoulders. These positions change a woman from a woman into a hole; her clitoris is out of the running and doesn't get anything but air. Remember the all too apt description of copulating women in that best-selling novel *The Chapman Report:* "Like beetles on their backs." I've often thought that one reason many women have trouble coming is that they feel so *ridiculous* in some of the positions men put them into.

To climax, a woman must first feel lovely and sexy. She does if she's undulating in a sinuous twist, but not when she's bouncing up and down like a ball.

• Don't speed up when she starts to moan. The reason she started to moan in the first place is that what you were doing *then* felt good.

• Don't ask questions that require silly answers.

The most irritating man is the one who, when he does something that obviously delights the girl, asks her: "Does that feel good?" What can she say except yes? Saying yes or no at a time like that makes a woman feel ridiculously inarticulate; this, in turn, makes her feel honor-bound to follow it up with a colorful and well-turned phrase. Usually, she will fail, because it's hard to word things well at a time like that.

Other cross-examinations of this kind? To cite just one example, there's the man who makes his girl writhe like a snake in heat by sucking her nipples while they have intercourse. When he rouses her to a complete pitch of passion, he stops what he's doing and asks: "Would you like me to suck your nipples?" In other words, "Should I do what I'm doing?" Why ask a question that's already been answered by action, especially when the asking interrupts and spoils the action?

The Right Way to Do Wrong

Here are two variations on the basic missionary position that will aid a woman in coming:

• The "schoolgirl twist." This is the missionary position as practiced, of necessity, in the back seat of cars. To keep from tumbling off the narrow seat, the woman twines her legs around the man's. On the back seat or in bed, it forces the couple's crotches even closer and sets up a delicious friction. It also provides the woman with more leverage; she can use the man's legs to pull on as she undulates, and at the same time keep him where she wants him. (Maybe it's called the schoolgirl twist because twined legs look like braids—but I doubt it.)

• Let her do *all* the work. I realize this is asking a lot of the male ego, but it's not something you do all the time, and the benefits a man reaps from an ecstatic woman will make him feel like a king.

After the man has pushed his penis into his partner's vagina as deeply as possible, he should keep perfectly still while the woman, with knees bent and heels pressed firmly into the mattress, raises her hips enough to permit her to thrust freely up and down.

For the woman who has difficulty reaching orgasm, this technique has an immense psychological advantage. A motionless man reduces her anxiety; because he *seems* unexcited, she won't worry as much that he will come too quickly for her. Also, exchanging traditional sex roles— the male becoming "passive," like the proverbial Victorian woman who believed that "ladies don't move"—helps the nonorgasmic woman to slip naturally into aggressive sexual behavior. *Somebody* has to move, and if he doesn't, then it's up to her. This is psychologically ideal for the woman who yearns to be aggressive but who doesn't enjoy the woman-on-top position either physically or emotionally. By doing all the work in the missionary position, she has it both ways.

It's also very good for her man. He gets the thrusts and pulls he likes, yet his passivity allows him to feel what's going on inside of her better. He also gets a rest if he's been overexerting himself lately. The ridges of her vaginal walls and the gush of her juices are more discernible to him when he keeps still. He has it both ways psychologically, too: he's on top, yet he's having an incredible sexual experience without moving a muscle!

Female Foibles

SLY QUESTIONS—FEMALE STYLE

• "Do you love me?" She *knows* he's going to say yes (whether he means it or not). Does she honestly expect him to say no? And besides, what does "love" mean? As you know, there's no easy definition for it. So what good does it do to ask, especially at a moment like this? (A variation on this is "*Say* it! *Say* it!")

• "Do you *really* want me?" This is comparable to dragging a decapitated body from an auto wreck and asking "Are you hurt?" After all, he's making love to her, isn't he? What more can he do?

• Two real beauts are: "Promise you'll wait for me?" and "Are you coming yet?" If he's a halfway considerate guy, he's probably trying to concentrate on the multiplication tables or yesterday's baseball scores, so why remind him of what he's trying to forget? And if he's having trouble getting there, don't remind him of *that*, either.

• "Am I *good* for you?" This is found on page 331 of *Peyton Place*, published in 1956. An unfortunate number of women have picked up on it, and an equal number of unfortunate men are sick of hearing Constance MacKenzie's bat-brained question.

• Most women know that men have a great deal of sensation in the anus. This is an easy place for her to fiddle with in the missionary position, and so she does. However, when she reaches down, separates his cheeks, and sticks her finger between them, she has been known to ask, "Here?"
Where else?

• "Can you *feel* me?" This is a favorite of women who have labored long and hard over the vaginal-squeezing exercises that have recently been described in so many magazines. Now that she's mastered the technique, she wants *compliments*.

This is really the least silly of the silly questions. If she's still learning, calling a man's attention to her first efforts will—if she gets an honest answer—at least let her know whether she's making any progress down there.

You Can Be Too Feminine

Some women feel that sex is basically a man's job and see it as a slam-bang business full of grunts and violent movements. These aspects of it make many women think it would be wrong to "compete" with the man, and so they try to infuse femininity into the act by doing sweet, graceful things that most men really don't care about. Running her hands through his hair, fondling the back of his neck, and trailing feathery-light fingertips down his back and ribs are some of the ploys women use. This sort of thing can be good or bad, depending on the moment and the man. But it's a rare man, and not much of one either, who responds to the woman who associates femininity with maternity and bestows fond pats on, and utters maternal coos and comments to, her man while they're making love. He's no baby; if that's what she wants, then she should have one.

Remember that although intercourse is the ultimate sexual act, ironically there are no sexes in bed. Both partners are glorious human animals at such a time. That's why overplaying the femininity game, and especially the maternal bit, is psychologically wrong.

You women out there should forget about that "You Tarzan, me Jane" nonsense. Be as aggressive as you want. Go after his ear and give it a thorough tonguing. Squeeze his buttocks and play with his balls. Give as good as you get!

Again, I'll quote Germaine Greer, this time on too-feminine bed behavior. What men really crave, she says, is "some straight dirt, some gusto in the business." I say amen to that, because doesn't giving him what he craves get you a lot of what *you* crave, too?

4. The Big Bang; or The Making of an Orgasm

Back in the days of strict censorship, an editor once advised the author of a sexy novel, "There are two things that can't be described; one of them is a sunset."

Prevented from calling a spade a spade, writers tried to describe the female orgasm with romantic euphemisms, such as: "She soared into an infinity of delight" . . . "She sailed on a golden cloud" . . . and even, believe it or not, "Her thighs wept."

Nowadays we can say what we mean. But that doesn't mean we've left all of our hang-ups and outmoded attitudes behind. Whatever it's called—coming, going over the top, the big bang, climaxing, peaking—we make it sound like an insurmountable task, like climbing a mountain. I believe this is why so many women can't do it.

I get hundreds of letters every week. One of my more intellectual correspondents called my attention to a lovely way of thinking about orgasm that she found in the French translation of Mary McCarthy's novel *The Group*. In the English version, the man says to the girl, "You came," but in the French he says (and note that he doesn't use the familiar "*tu*") , "*Vous avez joui*," which translates literally as, "You played." One of the reasons people have trouble playing the orgasm game is that they're trying to play by the wrong set of rules. No wonder it sometimes seems more like work than play. First let me dispel some of the lies and misconceptions so many people use as rules. Then I'll give you a new set of no-rule rules to play by.

Coming Through the Lie

Here are some of the most frequent lies about orgasm that men and women tell one another, not to mention themselves:

• Any woman can come if the man lasts long enough. This is partially true—but it takes the fun out of it for all concerned. The most intense orgasms usually happen during the first five minutes. The twenty minutes to half an hour of steady pumping that many men strive for tend to make a woman feel like she's being serviced in a machine shop. She'll probably eventually come, yes, but it will be an "almost-but-not-quite" orgasm. Technically it's an orgasm, but realistically it's a faint flutter that leaves her more frustrated than if she had had nothing at all. The answer here might be more foreplay. Just remember what Hamlet almost said: The foreplay's the thing. . . .

• When a woman starts to come, a man should start thrusting as hard as possible. No! Just the opposite; he should keep almost still. If he does, they

will both have a better time. I've received countless letters from women who ask why their masturbatory orgasms are so much more intense than
those they have during intercourse. The reason is
that during masturbation a woman can feel the
contractions in her vagina because she lightens her
touch when she feels her climax start.

A man who starts to pound his partner unmer-
cifully as soon as she begins coming is, in a way,
doing to her vagina what we do to our nose when
we stop a sneeze by pressing hard with a finger on
the upper lip.

On the other hand, keeping relatively still for
her, though letting her know he's still in the ball
game with a gentle, rhythmic thrust, will not only
enable *her* to savor her throbbing vagina, but *he*
will be able to feel it, too. A pummeling penis
can't feel much of anything except its own sensations.

● *"I'll give you an orgasm!"* One of the chief
problems of the sexual revolution is that too many
men, knowing that a woman is now *supposed* to
have an orgasm, take verbal responsibility for it
before they even get into bed. Promising her a
sexual rose garden is negative salesmanship. The
power to give implies the power to take away. Not
only that, but when a man places the responsibility on himself, he immediately becomes tense and
wonders if he'll really be able to deliver the
goods. His tension is transmitted to his partner,
with the result that both of them end up making
love to his masculine image instead of each other.

Remember, it's *her* orgasm. And she isn't giving
one. She *has* one.

• Simultaneous orgasms are best. Again, no! Coming together is something that everyone ought to experience, for the experience, and it will occasionally happen to lovers who know each other well and have slept together many times. Otherwise, it's better if the woman has hers first.

Many men think that "finishing without her" makes a woman feel used, and others feel that once a woman has come herself, she immediately loses all interest in the proceedings.

Both of these attitudes are wrong. A satisfied woman can relax and enjoy a man's strong pumping. A still-tingling vagina is more sensitive to penile pulsations than one struggling toward its own climax. A woman who has had her own orgasm can concentrate on feeling that ready-to-come penis swell inside her just before climax, and she'll know the exact second when the next spurt begins. Feeling a man come inside her can be the most thrilling thing that can happen to a woman.

Some men also think that it hurts a woman if they continue thrusting after she's come, but that's a misconception, too, stemming from the fact that a man's penis is tender and sensitive for several minutes after ejaculation; women, however, are emotionally and physically different. As I said before, once a woman has had her own orgasm, she can enjoy her increased sensitivity to her man. And believe me, she'll be feeling no pain. She may even want to indulge in the additional psychological satisfaction of a fantasy—such as being "taken," as the Victorians used to say.

Finally, a woman who has come can enjoy watching her man's face when he comes. This is also a time for her to do what many women secretly crave to do: talk dirty. Now that she has come and can think straight again, she *can* manage a colorful, well-turned phrase.

And then, of course, after the woman has had her turn at bat and is on second base, she just may enjoy the dividend of coming all the way home while her partner is still happily en route to first base. (If this sounds mixed up, don't be too tough on me. What does an unsophisticated Dutch girl know about the American sport of baseball?)

"Her Breath Came in Short Pants"

This is my favorite line from a porn novel I once read. It says a great deal about why so many women have trouble coming: they hold their breath when they feel orgasm approaching. Any strong emotion causes people to hold their breath; we all do it instinctively whenever we're frightened or surprised. Some women have an unconscious orgasm phobia—indicated by that not uncommon exclamation, "It's a little like dying!" They associate orgasmic throes with what they imagine death throes to be like, and this creates anxiety that leads them to hold their breath.

Regular, rhythmic breathing is relaxing in any intense situation. Ideally, orgasm should and can be like breathing—that is, something we can't help doing. Breathe as deeply as possible, then let it out with an abandoned panting sound. If it looks like an orgasm, feels like an orgasm, and sounds like an orgasm, chances are it *is* an orgasm.

The Orgasmic Cramp

One of the hardest things for men to understand is that some women need an orgasm to relieve menstrual cramps. On the first day of the menstrual period, when cramps are generally most severe, many women will masturbate even if they don't indulge in auto-eroticism at other, more pleasant times. What men can't understand is how a woman can have sexual pleasure while she's in glandularly induced pain. It has nothing to do with masochistic perversity, as some men believe. It's a well-documented fact that women reach a peak of sexual receptivity at or near the time of menstruation, and the worse the cramps, the more a woman's concentration is centered on her pelvis. Cramps are a grinding ache that throbs rhythmically, so that it feels almost as if her heart is down there. There comes a point when an intense feeling is an intense feeling is an intense feeling—which is why many women who have difficulty reaching orgasm can reach one effortlessly and quickly during cramps.

A man who becomes a "good Samaritan" to his woman when she has cramps by masturbating her will often reap rewards in bed later that month. All he has to do is wet his index finger with saliva or jelly and tease her clitoris into an orgasm.

Faking It

Honor-bright purists and some feminists say a woman should never do this, but I happen to disagree. Most women fake once in a while. Certainly, faking is a much better method than resorting to those famous last words: "Never mind, it doesn't matter, go ahead."

If you're going to fake, ladies, make sure you do it right. Don't grin. Remember, an orgasm is more like a convulsion than anything else, and nobody grins when he's having a fit. Go stiff, tighten your hips and buttocks, arch your back, and grimace with bared teeth as if you were just breaking the tape in the Olympic hundred-meter dash.

As for what you should say when you're faking, you'll sound like a porn-novel heroine if you come out with, "Yes! Yes! Yes! Yes! Yes! Yes!"

Don't labor the point. The reason porn heroines do this is that the writer is desperate to finish the book as quickly as possible and get the check; six yeses take up a whole line and help the writer get to the bottom of the page in jig time.

Any more lengthy porn monologue is out, too. Nobody who was really coming could keep it all straight. The rule of thumb is: if you have to memorize it, forget it.

Repairing the Damage

Suppose a woman didn't come and didn't fake? Most of you men want to help, and one obvious solution is to substitute a finger for that no-longer-rigid lower digit.

Begin right away, as soon as the penis is out of the vagina. A woman who is still excited can take at least two fingers. Use the index and second fingers, while keeping your thumb revolving lightly over her clitoris. If you have an especially big thumb, it will feel more like a penis than one or more fingers. Push it into her vagina, then insert your index finger in her rectum. When both are all the way in, pinch them gently together so that she'll experience a tugging feeling in the thin wall of flesh that separates vagina and lower bowel. Thrust thumb and then finger, taking turns in a pistoning movement, first one and then the other. While you are doing this, lick her clitoris. It won't be long now.

Did He Come?

This is seldom a problem, but it does happen. A man can simply lose his erection inside the vagina. Usually it's because he's fatigued; sometimes it's a psychological reaction to any number of things which may or may not have anything to do with the woman. Failure to come is called anorgasm, to use the medical term for it.

The extreme cause of anorgasm in men is priapism—named for the Greek god Priapus, who went around with a perpetual erection. Priapism is not a blessing but a curse, a painful medical problem that, fortunately, is rare.

There are, however, different kinds of orgasm in men. When described clinically, all of them sound like convulsions to one degree or another, but an orgasm is, after all, an intense reaction—to pleasure.

According to Dr. Alfred C. Kinsey, about twenty percent of men have mild climaxes, with very little penile pulsation, and a dribble instead of a spurt.

Forty-five percent of men become rigid overall, with "twitching of one or both legs, of the mouth, of the arms, or of other parts of the body."

About seventeen percent experience knotted leg muscles, spasmodic twitching, staring eyes, and violent jerking of the penis.

Five percent become "frenzied" and have hysterical reactions, including talking and laughing.

The remainder experience "extreme trembling, collapse, loss of color, and sometime fainting." Others may scream and suffer excruciating pain if the movement is continued after ejaculation or if the penis is even touched slightly.

Which is best? It doesn't make the slightest difference, since men obviously have little control over their orgasmic response. I'm just telling you which group you (or you partner, if you're a woman) fit into, in case you're curious.

A woman should remember that a man takes

great delight in "filling her up." Don't be too quick to jump out of bed and run to the bathroom, even if you do feel sticky and are worried about the sheets. Keep a towel handy beside the bed and spread it under you. Needing to do this flatters a man.

Many women who use diaphragms are especially punctilious—and tactless—about "cleaning up" afterward. Never use this expression to a man, for it implies that what he poured into you is dirty.

People in polite society, up until about two or three decades ago, didn't talk much about orgasms. They were secret, "forbidden" experiences for virtually all women and for quite a few men, according to the puritan code that still had a stranglehold on our society's sexuality.

Even in today's "liberated" atmosphere, the most famous orgasm of our time comes to us from the thirties—the days of the Spanish Civil War, when radicals and revolutionaries all over the world went to fight the good fight against fascism. It was then, as depicted in Hemingway's best-selling novel (and film) *For Whom the Bell Tolls*, that the Spanish heroine, Maria, told the American hero, Robert, how it truly felt: "The earth moved!"

Xaviera's message for the seventies: "Earth Movers of the World, Unite—in Carnal Knowledge!"

5. The Power of Positive Positioning

Needless to say, I believe in being sexually free and spontaneous at all times. Good bed sport demands it, and besides, it's fun to use your imagination and realize your fantasies, even when they turn out to be something less than the super sexperience you dreamed of.

Nothing is more provocative, or just plain sexy, than trying different positions, as long as you keep a firm grip on your sense of the ridiculous and realize that there are only a few *basic* variations. There are enough of these, however, to keep everyone feeling happily experimental. The rest—that is, the other thousand or so—are "pseudo" positions, minor variants that don't necessarily add anything in physical pleasure, although some of them might add emotional pleasure if they help you live out your erotic fantasies.

Generally speaking, I think a position is a mistake if you have to work at it. It's also a mistake if either partner utters any of the following:

"Goddamnit!"

"Oh, wait, wait, wait!"

"Will you for Chrissake get off my foot!"

"Well, you *said* that's what you wanted."

"Darling, I can't breathe."

"Is it in?"

"Is it in *what?*"

There's no position you can think of that's really new, and it wasn't our sexual revolution that first tripped off interest in positions, not by many centuries of doing what comes naturally, and unnaturally. There have been other sexual revolutions, you know, and one of the wildest occurred in ancient Rome. The Roman poet Ovid had a great deal to say about different positions. Aesthetics were an important element of sexual pleasure in Ovid's day, as they should be in ours, and he based his position theories on which positions would show off a woman's best features.

Here is part of what he wrote:

Recline your face upward, you who're fair
  of face;
Display your back, whose back's your chiefest
  grace;
Well-shaped legs on shoulders should be laid;
Hector's bride was far too tall to sit her
  horse astride;
Youthful thighs and faultless breasts demand
That you lie slantwise and your lover stand.

Considering the problems of rhyme and meter, this is not bad advice—as far as it goes. However, it's not only a woman's best points but also her mood, and that of her lover, that dictate what position they will choose for any given moment.

"Put It in for Me"

There's hardly a man in the world who has not made this request. Even men who claim they hate "aggressive" women will ask their bedmates to perform this most aggressive of all sexual acts.

The ideal position for female insertion is the woman above the man. Not only can she get hold of his penis without crushing her hand, but her lover can *see* what is undoubtedly the world's most fascinating disappearing act.

This position is popularly known as "sitting on it"—but please *don't!* At least, not all the way all at once. In the first place, it can be uncomfortable for a man who has an unusually sensitive glans. Moreover, it's psychologically unpleasant for both partners. No woman wants to behave like a mindless pile driver at a time like this, and while female spies have been known to hide things in their vaginas, there is absolutely nothing contraband about a penis—you can even take one into Turkey. . .

It's much better to prolong genital sensitivity by making female insertion last as long as possible. Instead of squatting over your man, straddle him gracefully. Slowly spread your legs wide around his body—if you're especially supple, you can do a ballet split—and ease yourself down over his crotch, remembering to keep your back straight and your breats thrust out. (Don't hunch. Remember Ovid's advice about showing off your best points.)

You can play "look, no hands" if your man has a penis that points straight up when erect, but not all men do. Some hard-ons lie along the thigh, or lie back on the stomach. In either case, don't be too quick to tuck it away; you can increase the chances of orgasm (for both of you) if you first massage your vulva and clitoris with his well-swollen head. If it stands alone, put your hands on your hips and do some sexy bumps and grinds against it while you fantasize yourself as a stripper. If you have to hold it, as will probably be the case, take it in your thumb and forefinger and guide it into yourself, making sure you keep your thumb moving on the underside of his foreskin to give him added pleasure.

Women who have most of their sensitivity in the vestibule of the vagina may especially enjoy the woman-above position because it enables them to be stimulated by the head alone. They claim "it's the first inch that counts; everything else is surplus." It's asking too much of any man to insert only his penis head, but in the woman-above position, he has no choice; you are the fuck*er* and he is the fuck*ee*. So enjoy, enjoy!

If a man is extremely big, the woman-above position is actually preferable to any other, because the woman can regulate what might otherwise be a painful insertion. With really well-hung guys, it's a good idea for the woman to climb aboard and insert his penis into herself while it's still soft. No matter how big it is, a relaxed penis is easy to work in; then you can both enjoy the exquisite sensation of feeling it grow inside you. Believe me, there's nothing better than getting "filled up" in this way.

When the woman is in the saddle, it's much easier for her lover to masturbate her clitoris, or for her to masturbate herself. Most men are turned on when they see a woman playing with herself; far from being a reflection on his ability to satisfy you, it's a way of telling him that he's gotten you so hot you can't keep your hands off yourself. You can also play with your nipples in the woman-above position, or he can reach forward and roll them between thumb and forefinger in time to your pumping rhythm.

If your man has an especially long penis that tends to tilt up toward his stomach, you can achieve the most intense clitoral pressure possible by lying flat on top of him with you legs closed tightly and stretched out between his. But make sure it's long; otherwise it will fall out and you'll both be shortchanged.

Maybe the best reason for a woman to get on top is that is enables her to "take full measure of her man." *Seeing* a penis is just as thrilling as feeling it.

Not All Desk Jobs Are Dull

It's hard to get through college without experiencing this one. The liabilities, according to a coed friend of mine, are obvious but minor: Phi Beta Kappa keys dangling on your bare stomach; the imprint of a spiral notebook on your back; and ink smudges from all the news that's fit to print on unprintable places.

If college didn't prepare you for a desk in the

workday world, you can always learn on the job. According to a friend of mine, her willingness to pick up new skills has paid off. She screws her boss every evening and puts it down as overtime.

Nothing can beat a "desk job" for leverage. The man is flat on his feet and can pump away for all he's worth without worrying about supporting himself, holding on to anything, or losing his rhythm because of twisted bedcovers or a too-soft mattress. The woman is seated on the edge of the desk, legs spread wide. The man can reach her clitoris easily, and best of all, he can gaze down to his heart's content at the sight of his penis sliding in and out of her vagina—a visual turn-on that all men crave.

The standard desk is also an ideal height, because it is just slightly less than crotch-high when measured against the average man. Add a woman, and everything is in exactly the right place.

Desk jobs are also ideal quickies. Very little undressing is required on the part of the woman, the man merely has to unzip. Another benefit of this position is women find it easy to climax because the most natural thing for a man to do is to use his fingers on the clitoris. (There isn't much else he can do with his hands unless he wants to salute the flag.) Also, if he keep his pants on, most materials set up a pleasant, scratchy feeling against the woman's anal region.

It's best not to use this position if you're employed by the civil service, where bureaucrats like to affix signs to things. There just might be a sign reading: "Anything screwed on this desk is the property of the U.S. Government."

Doggy Bone

Many people object to the all-fours position because it's so impersonal. Lovers should and do enjoy looking at each other, but there are times when even the most devoted couple is motivated by sheer lust rather than by tenderer feelings. This is an ideal time to use the doggy bone.

It's also a logical position for people who are not at all in love but who find themselves in bed together. From time to time, most of us meet someone whom we might not want to have a relationship with but whom we simply *must* bed—if only once. The animality that drives us on such occasions is no cause for guilt; it's just one particular kind of sex to which none of us is immune. And it can be quite thrilling in its own special way.

These are the more complex reasons for using the doggy bone. There are simple ones, too: because it's fun, because it's different, and because it's instinctual. After all, our ancestors did it this way.

Obviously, ass men like it, and so do women who have unusually sensitive behinds. It's just about the most sensible and safe position to use during pregnancy, too.

The advantages are many. The breasts are more sensitive to touch when they hang down and swing freely, and they are easy to reach. The woman can enjoy both vaginal and clitoral stimulation by placing a pillow under her crotch and rubbing against it as she arches her back up to her partner. Instead of using a bed pillow with a smooth case, try a sofa pillow with a rough nubby cover, such as tweed or corduroy, for more intense feeling. (But please remember not to put the same pillow back on the sofa. Callers such as ministers, Avon ladies, and mothers will get upset.)

A variation on the standard doggy bone is the "lap dog." The man sits up in bed with his back against the headboard while the woman straddles his lap and leans forward on her hands, looking toward his feet. If you hear someone singing "How Much Is that Doggy in the Window?" you'll know you left the curtains open again.

Was Whistler's Mother Trying to Tell Us Something?

The rocking chair, despite its homey image, is an ideal place to have sex. Many children experience their first sexual feelings on hobbyhorses, and the rocking motion was vital to the Japanese women who first used Ben-Wah balls centuries ago. (I'll tell you all about Ben-Wah balls in a later chapter.) Rocking is pleasant and sexy in and of itself, which is why mothers rock babies to soothe them.

Obviously, an armless rocking chair is preferable. The woman sits facing the man, and places her feet on the rungs. If you prefer to put your feet flat on the floor, wear shoes; otherwise, your little toesies might get rocked on. The last thing this version of "Rock-a-Bye Baby" will do is put you to sleep.

Last Tangle in Paris

Then, of course, there's the position made famous by Marlon Brando and Maria Schneider in *Last Tango.* I'm not referring to the position in which Marlon used up all that good butter. We'll come to that later in a special chapter in backdoor sex. I'm talking about the position in which they looked as if they were rowing—but they weren't.

The couple sits facing each other with knees drawn up; the woman drapes her thighs over her man's; both lean back on their arms, elbows stiff, as he dips his oar into her stream.

The drawback to this position is the drawback. You can thrust but you can't pull back very easily. It's psychologically sexy because you can both look down and watch your crotches, but it's hard on the behind to go scooting across the floor of an unfurnished apartment.

I find that the Last Tangle works best in a king-size bed with a very hard mattress. Ideally, the bed should be one of those old-fashioned brass types with sturdy bars. The man grabs onto the bars so he can, as the song says, row, row, row.

The Rape of Morpheus

It's possible to have sex while asleep, or at least to start out that way. As many couples have discovered, cuddling in the "stacked-spoon" position in a cold dawn has led to other things than generating a bit of mutual warmth.

The front-to-back side position, while not allowing for much vigorous movement, is ideal for winter temperatures when it's too cold to throw off the blankets. I especially like it early in the morning after a night of more lively lovemaking: you both have one more in you but you're too tired to do a slam-bang job of it.

This position is especially good when a man wakes up in the middle of the night wanting sex desperately, perhaps because of a dream he has had. Often he is reluctant to wake his woman up. If he's lucky, she'll be sleeping with her back to him, in which case he needn't wake her up. He can simply "spoon," as they used to say. Roll over onto your side, flip up the back of her nightgown if she's wearing one, and sneak it into her.

Many women object to this because they claim they feel "used." No one should ever "use" another person sexually, but every woman needs to realize that no matter how much a man values female sexual response, there are times when he needs a totally passive woman. Perhaps his ego is at a low ebb that day; there are many reasons why a man sometimes needs quick, silent, no-argument, unfancy sex. All you need do to accommodate him is to hunch up a little bit while you keep on half-snoozing.

Narcissism, with Mirrors

Turnabout is fair play; now it's time for women
to take their pleasure without considering the
man.

Sometimes it helps a woman to have an orgasm
if she can watch herself. This is hard to do in the
missionary position, when all you can see in the
bedroom mirror is your lover's behind and your
own feet.

A good way to star in your own private porno
flick is to place a big mirror opposite the foot of
the bed. Kneel astride your man with your back
toward him. Pay no attention to him whatsoever;
concentrate on the sight of your rise and fall in
the mirror. Play with your clitoris and nipples as
you witness the scene before you, as if you were
the director of an imaginary stag film. Pretend
that your lover is nothing but penis, balls, and a
pair of legs—the only parts of him that you can
see. Drown in your own erotic image, with no
thought for anyone but yourself. This might be
called "creative selfishness"; it's especially liber-
ating for the overly sacrificial sort of woman who
has been trained to think of the man's pleasure
before her own.

Female narcissism has been encouraged
throughout history, but for the wrong reasons and
in the wrong ways. Women have always been allowed to primp before mirrors while fully
clothed, but this is really antisexual narcissism. It
led to the kind of woman called a "clothes horse,"

and to the woman who "never has a hair out of place," and to the woman who dislikes sex because she's afraid of getting mussed up.

Sexy narcissism is making it with mirrors.

The Great Aching-Back Bang

This is a great position that I accidentally discovered while recovering from a muscle spasm in the lower back. The doctor told me to take the mattress off the bed and put it on the floor. So I did. He didn't say anything about abstinence. So I didn't bring it up.

I lay on my sore back with the bottom of my bottom flush with the end of the mattress. My lover knelt between my legs, and I placed my feet flat on the floor around him. The nap of the rug kept my feet from sliding, so I managed a great grip on things, with none of the usual slipping that occurs when you press your feet into a smooth sheet. I couldn't hump or wiggle, due to my bad back, but I could strain forward into my man's crotch and mash myself against him while he thrust into me. Sensational!

The Rack

This isn't quite as torturous as it sounds, unless you want to call it exquisite torture.

A woman can easily identify with Botticelli's famous painting of Venus rising from the sea. All women feel especially lovely when stepping out of the tub because they know they are fresh, clean, and sweet-smelling, and the bathroom affords two wonderful props for sex—the towel rack and the john.

However, we don't want to *tell* our lovers to come in at this time because that ruins the surprise element. Leave the door ajar so he'll know he has a green light. If he doesn't take the hint, leave it wide open.

A man should walk in, strip, step into the tub, and launch his "surprise" on the crest of a wave. The best position is a standing-rear one, with both partners gripping the towel rack. (Screw this in tightly before you screw anything else, and be sure you have a no-slip rubber mat on the tub bottom, or you might land on yours.)

If you're not finished by the time the water has drained away, adjourn to the john. This is not an unaesthetic trysting place if the lid is down and there's an attractive, fluffy cover on it, and when closed, it's the perfect height.

One of my best bathroom bouts was with a very tall man who perched me on the edge of the sink and plowed away merrily. (I carefully avoided gripping the hot-water faucet while all this was going on.) It was a perfect fit, and what you might call "plumbing the depths."

"As He Wheeled His Wheelbarrow ..."

You may remember doing *something* like this as a child, but you'll need a child's agility and sense of fun to enjoy it. In this one, the man stands up and holds the woman's thighs around his hips while she faces the floor and supports herself on her hands. Yes, it's "the wheelbarrow." This little trick is good for a minute or so, just for the hell of it, but it's rough going for all but Barnum & Bailey employees.

It's also disastrous for the couple without a sense of humor. Once upon a time, a husband talked his wife into trying the wheelbarrow. This particular woman was one of those spit-and-polish housekeepers who get upset whenever anyone puts his feet on a hassock. In the middle of their vigorous wheelbarrow sex, she spied some flecks of lint on her carpet and started picking them up then and there. She turned into a frigging vacuum cleaner, but neither of them cracked a smile. Maybe he should have dropped her right away instead of waiting for a divorce.

Basically, any position is fun as long as it's more or less within the realm of the sane. There will be some you'll try, only to burst out laughing in each other's faces—or wherever. This is good, for laughter is a vital ingredient in any intimate relationship, and it's often the chief language of love. After all, doesn't every couple have a favorite story about something outlandish that happened on their honeymoon?

Be daring. Be innovative. The best that can happen is that you'll discover a new route to ecstasy. The worst is that you'll have a good healthy laugh at yourselves together. And if you've learned anything from your friend Xaviera by now, you know that sex is much too important to be taken seriously.

6. Bottoms Up!
or a Short Course in Anal Intercourse

Everyone who wants to expand his erotic consciousness sooner or later finds himself thinking about that semiforbidden fruit, anal intercourse. But the way many people go about it is, to put it fittingly, ass-backwards. All sorts of negative emotions take over when people attempt, or even think about backdoor sex. So let's back up a moment and consider the subject objectively.

Chief among the blind spots is fear: of pain for women and of inflicting pain for men. Distaste and even revulsion are also common reactions, because many people are loath to associate sexual love with the area of our bodies that we use for defecation.

More of a mental barrier than a real one is the long arm of the law, both civil and religious. (Actually, of course, the "long arm" almost never interferes with the activities of the "short arm," as long as they're conducted discreetly and no minors are involved.) In many states, the only "legal" sexual contact is the penile-vaginal sex in the missionary position. Statutes condemn many very common sexual practices, such as oral-genital contact, but anal intercourse is the only form of "unnatural" sex that reaches all the way back to the

Bible for its name: sodomy. The fact that it's often associated with homeosexuality and bestiality makes it seem more of a crime than other practices that are merely lumped together under the catchall category of "abnormal."

Pornography and X-rated movies should come in for their share of criticism in the matter of anal intercourse, too. Both books and films give the erroneous impression that this form of sex is as easy as the front-to-front approach. The heroine invariably "takes it" with no trouble whatsoever; her lover disappears as effortlessly into her upturned rump as he does into her vagina; and she has a teeth-chattering orgasm after a few in-and-out movements. Viewers and readers who take all this at face value and casually take a fling at it often manage to shock themselves so badly that they are put off the entire idea from then on.

Current figures of speech do nothing to upgrade the image of the "Hershey bar," either. When you call someone an "ass," you're probably referring to an "asshole" rather than the four-legged beast. Either way, it's no compliment. All of us constantly use the expression "uptight" without stopping to think what it really means. It actually means "uptight *ass*," except that we leave off the "ass." Fear or the anticipation of pain, or even a general fear of the unknown, always makes us tighten the sphincter muscle that controls the anus, which in turn prevents us from having an embarrassing accident in moments of stress. It also seriously hampers ease of access when our experimentalists finally do get around to taking a fling at backdoor sex.

But despite the onus on the anus, many couples have discovered to their delight that there need be no tabus in lovemaking. Those who enjoy anal sex are those who approach it the way two mating porcupines approach each other—*very* carefully.

Boy, Have You Got the Wrong Number!

Apprehension over anal intercourse begins long before the physical part starts. Many men frighten women off unnecessarily by the way they broach the topic. The first hurdle in this particular game is to learn what *not* to say to get your partner to say yes. We're talking about the man popping the question, of course. If the woman invites the *man*, it's a shoo-in.

Most men wait until the very last minute, just before inserting the penis into the vagina during an ordinary love session, and then out it comes: "How about putting it in your ass this time?" A woman's first reaction is usually one of severe fright: she thinks he's going to *make* her do it. After all, there are only about two inches between the vagina and the rectum; all he has to do is aim down instead of up.

Another bad beginning is: "Did you ever have one in your ass?" If a woman says no, she's afraid she'll have some sort of virginal appeal and make him all the more insistent; if she says yes, she's giving her lover the green light regardless of what she may feel like doing *this* time. Maybe she's had anal intercourse once and hated it; maybe she's had it several times with another man and loved it. That doesn't mean that she wants to do it this particular time with this particular man—that is, with *you*. She could have several reasons, and not necessarily insulting ones. She might like it only with small men, and you're too big; she might prefer long thin penises in the back door and short thick ones up front—and, friend, you're thick. Or maybe she's simply bowel-conscious at this moment. (Don't forget that women have more trouble with this than men do because of premenstrual engorgement.) In any case, forcing her into a yes-or-no response will make her tense and guarded, and anal intercourse, more than any other sexual act, requires both physical *and psychological* relaxation.

Let Your Fingers Do the Talking

When in doubt, shut up. It's easy enough to find out if your woman is interested without saying a word. Like any other erogenous zone, the anus, both outside and inside, has varying degrees of sensitivity in different women.

In anal sex as in genital sex, foreplay is vital, so don't bungle your chances by being in too much of a hurry. Caress her buttocks thoroughly and see how she responds. Does she squeeze her cheeks hard? That means she's tensing up. Or do her cheeks dimple, ripple, and relax under your touch? That's a good sign.

Next, start at the base of her spine and trail your forefinger down her anal crevice. Does she push back against your finger and try to capture it between her buttocks? Does she roll over on her stomach invitingly when you begin to palpitate her rectum? If she does any of the above, your chances down below are improving.

It's a good idea to ease a woman into anal sex by making her progress analogous to her progress from virgin to nonvirgin in the realm of vaginal sex. Nearly every woman has experienced the fingerwork of a more-than-willing young suitor before she got to actual intercourse. So put her anus through the same logical steps.

A woman who has never had anything up her rear before should be treated the same way you would treat an up-front virgin. Don't shove your finger into her rectum simply because there's no hymen to worry about. Pretend that there *is* one. Lubricate your finger in her vaginal juices or with your own saliva. It's simpler to use these natural lubricants than suddenly to start fussing around with a tube of something. Basically, an inexperienced woman might make a panicky connection between your finger on her anus and the tube of K-Y jelly you bring to bed and thus conclude that you are planning to anally rape her.

For this initial test penetration, it's best to use your little finger. Your forefinger is welcome in a vagina, even a virginal one, but a virginal rectum is something else. Remember, you must be as *gradual* as possible.

Circle the wrinkled aperture of her anal rim rather than plunging straight in. You will soon know if she likes it, because she will work her sphincter muscle either to help draw it in for you or to exclude your finger. Sphincter muscles are very talented that way. When the tip of your finger is past the circle of musculature, don't begin to thrust as you would in her vagina—the thrill of anal lovemaking for a woman is not movement but an overwhelming feeling of *fullness*, of space being taken up, whether by a finger or by a penis.

Push your finger slowly in until you're knuckle-deep, then make slow, nonthrusting revolving motions with your entire wrist. Your last knuckle and the pad of your hand will set up an exciting kneading motion on her external rim and buttocks. This movement and pressure will be felt in her vagina, too, because the large colon is practically flush with her female sex organs.

While you're doing all this, make sure you're also doing something nonanal—kissing her nipples or tonguing her navel—to keep her from wondering what else you might have in store for her anally. The woman who enjoys each step of anal foreplay for its own sake will arrive more naturally at the "point of it all"—which is a bit of buggery, as the English say.

This Little Finger Went to Market

Now she's up to the hilt on your little finger, happily wriggling away—and protesting. The first time a woman gets a finger in the anus she's likely to squeal and say, "Oh, stop! You mustn't do that"—even while obviously enjoying every minute of it.

Little girls are raised to be dainty and fastidious—sometimes too much so. She's afraid that you'll run into something unromantic during your digital search and seizure, even though she undoubtedly took a thorough shower or bath before getting into bed and knows she's clean all over.

Set her mind at ease by obeying her instantly: take your finger out, but continue anal foreplay on the *outside*.

How? Rim her—that is, her anus. Gently, but firmly, around and around. Also, there's something soothing about a kiss, wherever it lands, even it it lands smack on . . . well, on the asshole.

Cheek-to-Jowl

Analingus is the Latin term for anus-plus-tongue. Some people call it "reaming," which comes from the Middle English *remen*, meaning to "open up." I suppose this is why the name of Harry Reems, the porno film star, is so easy to remember. The expression "rim" makes the most sense, because the anus wrinkles up into a rim. I call it around-the-world—not, of course, that I invented the phrase—because I do a thorough job of it when I'm the reamer, and I like a thorough job done to me when I'm the reamee. (I also like it to last a long time, like a world cruise on a slow boat.)

Uninitiated women call it "oh-that's-terrible!" At least until initiation day, when, with skillful guidance, they get to love it.

A woman should lie on her stomach with her legs opened wide and a pillow under her stomach to lift her up. Otherwise a man could get a crick in his neck. This position also affords you a glorious view of her nether charms. Spread her cheeks with your palms flat on each of her buttocks. Don't pull them open or else you'll forget yourself and pinch her when you get excited.

Lick leisurely up and down her anal crevice before you concentrate on her anus. Pay special attention to the perineum, the sinewy, dime-sized area of flesh between the vagina and the anus. This spot is extremely erogenous, and especially so in women who have had episiotomies—surgical incisions made during childbirth to widen the birth passage. The stitching-up process apparently does something nice to the nerve supply here. Incidentally, turn about being fair play, women should bear in mind (for some other moment) that the spot between a man's anus and what-would-be-his-vagina-if-he-had-one is also highly erogenous.

When you tongue her anus, circle your tongue rapidly, remembering to breathe hard so that your puffy breath will arouse her even more. *Do not chow down*—as with other erogenous zones previously discussed, less is more.

Obviously, this is a perfect time to lubricate her thoroughly with your saliva and excite her more at the same time. Yes, I know all this is *very* earthy lovemaking, but after all, aren't we all descended from people who originally came out of caves? The traditionally romantic approach is fine, but once in a while a man ought to play the gentle beast with his woman. He's more likely to be pleasantly surprised at the intensity of her response to this primitive passion, provided he follows the instructions in this chapter. A change of

pace and a change of place just might make her
turn on and light up as never before.

Many people consider rimming basically frustrating because the tongue can't really penetrate
very well. Of course, you can't blithely go sailing
all the way up to her transverse colon, but you *can*
insert the tip of your tongue just inside the sphincter muscle. An excited woman will help by
gripping on it and holding the tip inside her rectum for a few seconds—a new and novel two-way
sensation.

This Big Finger Went All the Way Home

By now your lover is relaxed and lubricated
well enough to take your forefinger. Go in with
gentle circular motions and pause each time she
grips or bears down to let her get accustomed to
the greater length and width. She will feel less
"speared" if she's lying on her side in a fetal position with her knees drawn up to her chest. This
position allows you to insert your thumb in her
vagina while you penetrate her anus; it's psychologically beneficial to give the "normal" orifice
some action while you're working your way into
the back door.

Once your finger is past the sphincter muscle,
don't take it out again. The sphincter is the Rubi-
con, and it will only get sorer with repeated
crossings. If she experiences discomfort, wait,
don't withdraw. Each back-to-the-beginning attempt will make her more nervous about her ability to take it.

The Fanny Club

Now that the subject of anal intercourse is being openly discussed, I should mention that most women feel a secret sense of rivalry with other women in this area, as in any other. They *want* to be able to take a penis in their rectum because it makes them feel equal to other women who can, and they want to be a better bedmate than those who can't.

A woman who succeeds as far as taking her man's biggest finger will probably want to go for the jackpot, but she'll worry about certain things. Her biggest worry is cleanliness; she doesn't want to "dirty" you, and she especially doesn't want to have to *see* the condition of your penis afterwards—just in case. To eliminate this pleasure-destroying fear, it's easier to use a condom than argue. The lubricated kind is best, but make sure you use still more professional lubrication. Vaseline and K-Y are better than baby oil because they are thick and gelatinous. Use plenty, both on your penis and in her anal area.

The woman should kneel with her chest touching her thighs; only an expert should get on top of her man. Kneel behind your companion's upturned buttocks, insert your penis between her cheeks, and press *gently* against her rim. Let the next movement be hers; ask her to push back against you as she revolves her hips in a screwing motion. As she does this, *lean*—do not thrust—forward.

Unless you are truly gargantuan, the tip of your penis should enter her rectum. Do not consider the battle won and proceed as you would in her vagina. Again, *wait*. The *pauses* in anal lovemaking are far more important than the active moments.

Keep up a steady stream of murmured encouragements to your partner, always assuring her that it's *her* show, that you will wait for her to make the next move. (This is one time when you shouldn't *stop* talking.)

Do *not* grip tightly on her hips, as this will make her feel trapped, and fearful that you will suddenly ram into her, using her hips as leverage. Instead, keep your hands busy in her crotch: if you excite her clitoris enough, she'll crave any kind of penetration.

Because the anus is much tighter than any vagina, a man doesn't need to thrust and pull in order to get his pleasure. The snugness alone is exciting enough, and the crowded conditions set up pulsations that the more elastic vagina does not give off. Also, there's a psychological stimulus that takes the place of more active movements by the man: merely knowing that you are actually there is perhaps the most powerful stimulus of all. This is still forbidden territory by conventional standards, and human nature is ever contrary.

The first few times you have anal intercourse, you may not get your penis all the way in. I can't emphasize the need for the gradual approach too much; it may take a week, a month, or longer before you can touch bottom. The important thing to remember is to let your success be cumulative—a woman who takes an inch tonight will probably want two inches next time.

Intermediate Inner Sanctum

Now that you're both used to the idea, you can take the rubber off and do something that resembles intercourse. Penile thrusts are possible in the female rectum, but remember she's not "an old queen," as the gay guys put it. A woman has smaller hands, feet, and everything than a man; she also has a smaller rectum. No matter how much she likes it, she can't take a hell-for-leather poke.

You *can* enjoy slow, easy thrusts, twisting motions, and *very* slow down-pulls. However, don't try to "hit the end" as you do in vaginal intercourse. The cervix is a tough, stubby, necklike organ, but intestines are more fragile.

It is also possible, with practice, to use other positions for anal intercourse. I once thought I was going to have regular vaginal intercourse with a customer of mine, but just before he penetrated me, he changed his mind and stuck it up my rectum. We were in the missionary position, and at first I thought I had been speared. Then, when the pain was excruciating, he pulled out for a while and then again thrust his penis back in. Suddenly, all the pain vanished and a delightful ready-to-come sensation spread over me. As it turned out, I did come, with a vibrating sensation, almost like a buzz—very different from the throbbing of a vagina in climax, but just as thrilling.

Later, the customer told me that he had practiced anal sex for years and found that the second insertion was comparatively painless for almost every woman he had ever known.

Ass-ercises, Anyone?

Unfortunately, there are no known exercises a woman can do to prepare herself for anal intercourse. I have heard gay men say that they stretch themselves with bananas and cucumbers, but I strongly advise against this—for either sex. The vagina is closed at one end, but the rectum is not: it keeps on going up. Things *can* get lost in there. By the time the doctor finds it and removes it, the damage could be serious.

Also remember that an ounce of prevention is worth an assful of cure. If you have hemorrhoids, which are as hard to bear as they are to spell, never even *consider* having anal intercourse. Buy some Preparation H and read a good book. Your horoscope, for example; see what the stars say about Uranus.

Finally, never go back and forth between rectum and vagina without washing the penis. Certain vaginal infections can be contracted through contact with fecal material.

Far from being a brutal form of sex, anal intercourse can be the most tender and considerate because it requires the utmost awareness of a woman's feelings and comfort, more than any other form of sex. The fact that some women keep trying to achieve anal pleasure despite initial pain is also proof of its erotic potential.

The appeal of virginity dies hard. Even today, many women who feel deeply for a man wish they could be virginal for him. You can't undo the past; if a man is number forty-six, there's no earthly way to make him number one. But it *is* possible to make him "first" if you've never had anal intercourse before. Many men find this just as flattering, if not more so, than being first up front, because it's proof of a complete trust and a free gift of something special. If a woman selects you to initiate her in this experience, you can take it as a high compliment. It means she thinks you're someone unique. Men might tell Satan, "Get thee behind me," but women reserve that suggestion only for someone on whom they want to confer a gift of themselves.

Remember everything I've told you—but most of all, remember the example of the mating porcupines.

7. Girl Meets Girl; or The Lore and Lure of Lesbianism

In the very first sentence of *Xaviera Hollander on the Best Part of a Man* I referred to myself as "a woman who has enjoyed love with both sexes." And so I have! But in this chapter I'm going to confine myself to love between woman and woman—with some *very* useful items of instruction for men along the way. And I'm going to begin with a quotation that one of my more literary lesbian lovers once called to my attention.

One of the original "feelthy" French novels is *Aphrodite* by Pierre Loüys, published in the 1880s. In what my friend tells me is a famous passage, the heroine, Chrysis, tells her rejected male lover, "A woman is a perfect instrument. From head to toe she's made solely and wonderfully for love. Only a woman knows how to love. Only a woman knows how to be loved. Therefore, if a couple is composed of two women, it's perfect; if it has only one woman, it's only half as good; if it has no woman at all, it's completely idiotic."

Basically, I'm more into men than women, and I consider myself a heterosexual, but there are times when I yearn for a woman in my bed. At those times, I agree with Chrysis.

Not too many years ago, whenever the subject

of lesbianism was raised, a straight woman might shudder and say, "Oh, I'd be revolted if a woman touched me!" What she didn't realize was that such a statement was an insult to herself; she was really saying that she found femininity, including her own, revolting.

Nowadays women have a higher opinion of themselves as people and have gained greatly in self-esteem. It's only natural, therefore, that they've begun to see each other in a different light—and often that light comes from the bedroom lamp.

The positive feelings women now have for one another, called "female bonding," have always existed. Women have always had extremely strong emotions toward members of their own sex. Unfortunately, these emotions often emerged negatively in the form of cattiness, jealousy, and gossip because women regarded one another as natural enemies in pursuit of the same prey—men. They developed the habit of close and critical mutual examination. They took in every detail of each other's figures, faces, and clothes in order to compare their own assets to those of their rivals. Naturally, this resulted in a high level of awareness of one another's sexual charms. For some brave and unconventional women, when those charms captivated them, it was only a hop, skip, and jump into bed together.

In today's franker atmosphere, it isn't necessary for women to be exceptionally brave or unconventional to want to experience lesbian love. They know that ego trips aren't for men only anymore; women are free to experiment with selfhood in the ultimate way—going to bed with someone physiologically like themselves. Some psychiatrists have classified lesbianism as a form of immaturity. They've probably read too many of those old-fashioned English schoolgirl novels, in which lesbianism is always thrown in somewhere between the hockey sticks and hot chocolate. In these novels, dewy little girls in tweed jumpers are always grabbing at each other and innocently wondering why it feels so good. Actually, lesbianism is a *very* grown-up woman's game.

Psychiatry also classifies lesbianism as a neurosis, but in my opinion it's just the opposite: a lesbian is a woman with an unusually healthy ego. Her lover is her mirror image; by what she does in bed she says, "This is me, and I am her." This is the highest form of female self-love.

Today's greater frankness has led to an increase in lesbianism in another way. Women constantly turn each other on with "verbal foreplay"—what used to be called "girl talk" in the days when it was more restrained. Now it would curl the hair of any man who happened to be eavesdropping. Men have always admitted that women are good at detail, and it's true. Two women talking about sex tell each other *everything*, and they often arouse each other in the bargain. When two horny people are alone, things start happening.

Widespread female interest in lesbianism is relatively new, but it's a well-known fact that this subject has always fascinated men. Lesbian sex shows and stag films have been a staple for years, and the reason is simple. Men will not admit how much in awe they are of their lesbian rivals, and this feeling is behind their fascination. They believe that lesbians have some mysterious and magical tricks guaranteed to turn women on, and they want to learn them.

They're right!

How to Get in Your Best Licks: Cunnilingus

In case you're wondering why I've said nothing so far in the earlier "heterosexual" chapters about the fine art of cunnilingus, it's because I think men can best learn this skill from lesbians.

Nearly every woman I've ever known has complained about how most men give head. All too often, it feels like circumcision *al dente*. Many men try to bite off more than they can chew—like the clitoris, the outer lips, the inner lips, or the whole business.

Another commom male fault is the bobbing head, as in bobbing for apples. Some men try to do too much all at once. They rub their noses against the clitoris in an effort to stimulate it; then they push their chins against the vaginal opening in a bizarre attempt at penetration. In a spirit of misplaced thoughtfulness, such men keep up a steady rhythm, but for all the good they do, they might as well turn on the bedside radio and tap their feet. Even if a man has just shaved, his chin is still rough; if he has a beard, as many men do nowadays, his woman will feel as if she's being made love to by a Brillo pad. As for his well-intentioned "nose job," it produces a head-on collision, not a caress.

A third male mistake proves the old adage "a little knowledge is a dangerous thing." Now that fifty million words have been written about the clitoris, men at last acknowledge its importance— but their recognition takes the form of overkill. Such men refer to cunnilingus as "sucking pussy" because that's exactly what they do, except they don't do it to the entire pussy—just the clitoris. *And they suck as hard as they can!* The only thing that will enlighten these men—and a fate they well deserve—is being forced to take a course in Latin. Perhaps then they will learn that *cunnus* means "vulva"—that is, the whole area—and *lingere* is the verb "to lick." If you were supposed to suck, it would be called "cunnisuckus," or something like that.

The fourth male mistake is comparable to talking with your mouth full at the table. They talk while they partake. They mean it in the nicest way; usually such a man wants to reassure his woman that she's sweet and delectable, but nothing distracts a woman more than a muffled voice drifting up from between her legs, saying, "Um-hmm! You taste good! Honey, I could eat you with a spoon." And so on. (Sometimes these men will raise their heads to speak, which makes the words audible—and the deed negligible.)

The fifth mistake is brevity. Many a man will hang in there for all of half a minute, then say, "Boy, are you wet! Let's go!" and jump into position for intercourse. Little does he know it's his own saliva, not her lubrication.

Lesbians know better. With few exceptions, most women, even confirmed lesbians, have been to bed with one or more men before they make love with another woman. They've been through all of the shenanigans described here and have learned from it what *not* to do when they encounter a delicious piece of nooky right under their own nose.

Here is how women do women: Place your woman on her back with a pillow under her hips. The longer your neck holds out, the longer the meal will last. She should spread her legs wide but keep them flat, the knees straight.

The vaginal lips open somewhat with the legs, but not enough for a really good session of cunnilingus. Gently spread them as wide as they will go, using both hands. Again I'll repeat what I said earlier about nipples: "Let the air get to it." That excited pink tissue is loaded with bristling nerve endings, and the clitoris is literally a bundle of nerves. Unlike exposed nerves in teeth, exposed clitoris nerves feel *good*. The spongy outer lips should be laid back. Remember, it's the clitoris that comes in for most of the fun, so find it and keep it out in the open.

Begin by licking lightly and quickly up and down the vulva slit—known as "tickling pink." The darting, vibratorlike tongue is much more pleasing than a slow, overthorough heavy tongue. The latter is the way a mother cat licks *real* pussies. This approach is the cat's meow only for cats.

Gradually confine your licking to the area around the clitoris. Circle it, always remembering to sneak up on it every so often rather than hitting it head-on. *Any* unbroken concentration directly on the clitoris, no matter how expert, will soon change pleasure to irritation, soreness, and eventually numbness.

When your woman begins to twist and moan, *don't let her come*. The joy of lesbianism is that neither partner has to worry about keeping an erection; women can go on all night, licking each other up to the point of no return, stopping, and then starting up again. The first rule of cunnilingus is: Eke it out.

To prevent her from coming too quickly, move away from the clitoris and circle your tongue around the opening of the vagina, prodding a little farther in each time. If your partner raises her legs and bends her knees back toward her chest, it's possible to wriggle your tongue in by as much as an inch. Very few women come from having a tongue inside, but this change of pace enables her clitoris to calm down before the next onslaught.

When she *does* come, hold her clitoris between your lips as lightly as possible so that you can feel the tiny pulsations that quiver through it. (This is hard to do, because by now she's thrashing all over the bed, but try it anyhow.)

69 Is Great, But 34-1/2 Is the Greatest

All lovers, whatever the sexual combination, love to try "sixty-nine" to see what it's like or to enjoy a slightly exotic change of viewpoint. But as a thoroughly satisfying mutual experience, it leaves something to be desired—namely, concentration. The best sex is built around creative selfishness, and it's almost impossible to give your partner an orgasm and concentrate on enjoying your own at the same time.

Heterosexual lovers have more problems than lesbians in this practice. It's dangerous for the

man to be on top, because he might thrust his
penis down too far into his woman's throat. Another problem is that there's often a considerable
difference in height between a woman and a man.
Lesbians don't have anything to choke anyone
with, and the height differential is generally con-
siderably less, so they get a little more out of
sixty-nine than straight lovers.

A favorite lesbian practice that anyone can enjoy might be called 34½. The lovers lie at opposite ends of the bed, one on top of the other.
(The sideways sixty-nine can be frustrating.) The
woman on top performs cunnilingus, while the
woman on the bottom rims her lover's rectum.
This way, the top woman gets intense stimulation
and a lot of pleasure but doesn't have to concentrate on her own orgasm while she brings off her
partner. I prefer 34½, and so do many other
women to whom I've taught it. Most of them say
that mutual cunnilingus is too crazy-making for
total enjoyment.

Bosom Buddies

No matter how much men admire various parts
of the female anatomy, in the last analysis it's the
vagina they're interested in. With lesbians it's the
breasts.

The reason for this is probably a mother-daugh-
ter fixation that is stronger in lesbians than in
other women, but I know from the letters I receive that women are more interested in breasts
than is generally believed. Some women who

don't want to "go all the way" with another
woman will often content themselves with breast
play and nothing more, resorting to masturbation
to complete the act.

A lot of women who are totally straight and
who don't desire any physical contact with wom-
en often have what amounts to a breast fetish.
They may never touch another woman's breasts,
but they fantasize about them and even excite
themselves with these thoughts while making
love with a man.

The best way to know what to do with breasts is
to have a pair of your own, so of course lesbians
are at an advantage. A favorite fondling technique
among women lovers is to use the flat of the palms
to brush the nipple as lightly as possible, back and
forth in a steady rhythm, using both palms at
once. (Once again, there's nothing to prevent a
man from emulating these techniques, which are
almost invariably more sensitive and considerate
than the ones men employ when left to their own
devices.) One woman kneels over the other and
reaches down, or she sits behind her partner and
holds her between her legs while she reaches
around.

Nipple-matching can turn a simple hug into
something very special. Boarding-school girls of
thirteen or so who have just sprouted breasts often do this and nothing more. It works best with
firm, conical breasts: thrust your chest out like a
soldier at attention and press your nipples into
those of your lover. (This one is a bit more difficult for a man to copy, but it can be done, in mod-
ified form.) When the nipples are matched up,
move lightly against each other. Or, one of you

can stand still while the other undulates, keeping the nipples touching as much as possible. It feels even better if you can coat both sets of nipples with slippery body lotion first.

Match the Snatches: Tribadism

Tribadism is the most elementary of all lesbian practices; the partners take the man-woman missionary position and rub their clitorises together to achieve simultaneous orgasm, or as nearly simultaneous as they can bring off.

The word "tribadism" comes from classical Greek and means, literally, "rubbing together." It was especially common, naturally, in Eastern harems. Many of these harems numbered their concubines in the hundreds, and a few select ones in the thousands. There was only one sultan, however. He would have had to make love every hour on the hour for an entire year before he got around to the same woman twice, so of course the bored harem members were as horny as students in an all-girl school.

Having nothing to do all day long but lie around and wait for another year to pass, the women turned to one another for sex. This turning might have been literal. As the famous harem painting by Ingres shows, the quarters were very crowded, so maybe the first tribadists discovered each other by accident. In all those acres of bare flesh, a reclining woman who turned over to ask her harem mate for a grape could easily have found herself lying on top of her friend. (Or maybe both Ingres and I exaggerate a bit.)

As a modern-day lesbian practice, tribadism is exciting but often frustrating and painful. It's virtually impossible to get two clitorises together in the missionary position. Worse, as sexual excitement mounts, the women tend to grind against each other, forgetting about the "mound of Venus"—a hard jutting bone—under that pretty, hair-covered hill.

Usually it's young or inexperienced lesbians who practice this kind of bump and grind. It's a favorite technique in girls' schools. Innocent teenagers who know just enough about heterosexual intercourse to know that the man gets on top and the woman lies under him logically but mistakenly assume that this is the only way for two women to make it.

They manage to brush clitorises for a few minutes, but they soon "lose touch," making both hornier than ever, as well as rather sore. The clitoris is just too concealed and tucked under for tribadism to be anything more than a very erotic introduction to another naked female body.

You *can* match snatches, but not in the missionary position. There are three ways to do it:

1. *S*waybacked but happy. Both women kneel facing each other, each with a pile of pillows behind her to lean into. Each sinks back into the pillows while keeping the pelvis upright and then they loop their thighs together, pressing their palms flat into the bed or rug for leverage. If one woman kneels against the wall, she can hold her own vulva open. Her lover leans into her while holding her own lips open.

2. Tabling the motion. One woman lies on her back on a table with her buttocks even with the edge, and spreads her vaginal lips wide with her fingers. Her lover stands between her legs and spreads her own lips, then steps forward. (This also requires a swaybacked stance.) If it's a wood table, remember to keep a can of Liquid Gold handy to remove the spots made by liquid silver.

3. "The scissors," or "hot cross bun." Imagine that you have an opened pair of scissors in each hand, the blades spread as wide as they will go. Bring the scissors together so that the apex of one pair is matched to the apex of the other. That's the position two women take for this version of tribadism.

One woman has to lie on her back while the other lies on her side, with their heads at opposite ends of the bed. Alternatively, both lie on their sides; in either position, they must join hands in order to pull against each other. Obviously, the clitorises are going to be turned in opposite directions, but believe me, it doesn't matter! There's enough pressure to bring both women off in a matter of minutes.

Once in a great while, it's possible for two experienced women to match up their vaginas and create a suction that sets up wild pulsations that feel just like a real vaginal orgasm. This is rare, but when it happens, it's heaven on earth!

Finger, Fingers—Or the Whole Hand

Even if a woman is exclusively lesbian and

wants nothing to do with men, she's a liar if she claims she has no interest in penetration. The vagina is *there*, and nature intended it to be filled; when it goes empty for too long, a woman can actually feel the emptiness in the most wrenching, melancholy way. It seems to stretch into an awareness of itself until she is conscious of an all-pervading hollowness that makes her feel empty all over.

A few lesbians are antimale purists; some others are what is called an "untouchable butch," meaning they like to do *all* the doing and never permit another woman to be dominant. These types are a very small minority, however. Nearly all lesbians poke around in and about each other, and they love every minute of it.

Lesbians have an advantage because a woman's hands are smaller, which means they can use more fingers for penetration. One female finger, unless the woman is nobly proportioned all over, will not even be felt; most couples use two, but even that is considered amateurish. The usual number is three, which suggests the Boy Scout salute but has a much lustier name. It's called a "cluster fuck" because three or four fingers must be clustered together for insertion.

The cluster can bring on a vaginal orgasm quicker than a penis because the thickest part of the cluster is at the base, where fingers meet the hand. The knuckles form a big knot in the vestibule of the vagina—approximately the first inch or so—where most of the nerve endings are located. (The interior of the vagina is virtually anesthetized.)

Three average-size female fingers clustered at

the knuckles are about the same width as a thick penis. Four fingers tightly grouped together are as wide as a real wing-dinger of a whang.

Rarely, when the doer has small hands and the do-ee has had one or more children (or has a large vagina), the whole hand will fit in wrist-deep. Again, remember our friends the porcupines; test-drive it first, go easy, and use plenty of lubrication. Fortunately, a woman, unlike a man, is so familiar with her own vagina and what it can take that she will know when to stop as well as when to start.

The big thrill in taking the whole hand up your vagina is feeling the pulse in your lover's wrist. This is especially delightful after you've come, and your lover leaves her hand inside you after you are both quiet and just lying there supersensitively. (Men with small hands take note: you have a priceless asset that should be put to use.)

The best thing about penetration with the fingers is that you can go on as long as you please. Fingers don't get soft. Arms do get tired, but you have two of them and so can switch around. The disadvantage of this practice is too much of a good thing. After the tender preliminaries are over, knowing that there is no possibility of pregnancy, loss of reputation, locker-room gossip, or the tension that results from the famous battle of the sexes, lesbians not only feel free but sometimes *too* free. When two women really get started on a sex binge, they tend to go at each other with no holds barred for hours at a stretch. Although there's more sweetness in lesbianism than in any other form of sex, there also can be more violence

at times. A man and a woman are always conscious
of the difference in their respective physical powers, but two women feel that their strength is
equal. Thus they tend not to be so careful as they
might in moments of sexual frenzy.

Dallying with Dildos

In my opinion, women who use dildos on each
other *all* the time really would prefer to have a
man. Dildos are for lesbians what French ticklers
are for heterosexuals—a fun thing, a sometime
thing to satisfy curiosity and, occasionally, to
provide a different kick.

Many women who have shed just enough hang-
ups to go to bed, finally, with another woman,
tend to shy away from a dildo as something unnatural and perverted. Going down on each other
seems natural and permissible because, after all,
that's the ultimate act women are equipped to
perform. A dildo "adds something" that nature
didn't bestow, thus making lesbianism less natural
and, somehow, more "lesbian."

If you want to use a dildo and your girlfriend is
reluctant, use it on her by hand first. Rather than
discuss it beforehand, just do it. Nonchalance is
often the best approach.

The biggest psychological problem that dildos
create is an optical illusion. A six-inch dildo is the
same size as the average penis, but it looks much
bigger because it's not attached to a large male
body. Reaching into a bureau drawer, holding up
a dildo, and saying to your girlfriend, "Look what

I bought for us!" is a good way to scare the bejesus out of her. It's better either to do the job by hand or to strap it on yourself and *then* make your announcement.

There are two special kinds of dildos made for lesbians. One is the double dildo, which is curved in the middle and has a penis head at both ends. Each partner, of course, inserts one end in her vagina, and they saw away merrily.

The other is a chin-strap model that allows you to perform intercourse and cunnilingus simultaneously. I have never used the chin-strap doubledipper, nor have I ever been on the receiving end of this model, but a friend who has experienced it says, "If you can keep a straight face, you're on *and* in." Above all, don't forget yourself and answer the do-ee while wearing your chin-strap dildo.

The most important thing to keep in mind about any dildo is that it's not part of your body; therefore, you can't feel what you're doing with it. It's undeniably thrilling for a woman to strap on a dildo and perform like a man—so thrilling that she might get carried away. If you bang too hard, you could hurt your lover without realizing it.

Another important caution: if you want to use a dildo, make sure it's a real dildo. Don't use substitutes, such as cucumbers, tool handles, or the like. They're not designed for the purpose, and someone could get hurt.

Meet Me at the Fountain of Love

As I said earlier, no one can agree on whether or not a woman ejaculates fluid at the moment of orgasm. Men would like to believe it happens, which is why porn novelists make it happen on every other page. Every sex manual I've ever read, both medical and popular, has claimed that there's no such thing as the "female spurt." They claim there's no such thing as a vaginal orgasm, too—but there is.

I'm here to tell you that the "female spurt" may be rare, but it *can* happen here. I only felt it happen once, when my fingers were up against a woman's cervix. Suddenly, her entire vagina swelled up like a balloon; the wrinkles smoothed out, and the flesh became stretchy and taut, like the insides of your cheeks when you blow them out.

She stopped moving and went stiff all over; then, from the area surrounding her cervix came a fine spray like a shower of hot needles. It lasted only a second, but I felt it. I imagine it would be impossible to feel it with a fast-moving penis, but you *can* feel it with a finger.

Just as thrilling to me was feeling her expand inside. If men are unfamiliar with this expansion, it's because few penises can last as long as a finger—almost an hour in our case. So try your finger sometime.

Bye-Bye, Butch

Now that women are becoming more aggressive at both work and play, the old "butch-femme" combo is dying out. I say good riddance, because it was a parody of the male-female relationship. It's also a stereotype, and I don't believe in any kind of stereotyping. It's no longer necessary for a woman with a naturally strong and dominant personality to dress, talk, look, and act like a man in order to express her strength. As the butch passes into history, the femme has naturally gone with her. Nowadays, most lesbians are attractive feminine women with whom any man would be proud to be seen.

Now that women are trusting one another more and are becoming true friends and companions, many of them will probably experiment with lesbian relations for the first time. Someday it may become almost inevitable, because, to a woman, giving pleasure is as important as getting it. Many men still don't realize that affection and fondling with or without orgasm is important to a woman; this is something that only another woman fully understands at this stage of our social development.

Today's woman is also beginning to realize her sensuality with a freedom never before open to her. In my opinion, the totally sensual woman is bound to be drawn to lesbianism, because she's no longer psychologically capable of denying one form of pleasure in favor of another. To such a woman, pleasure is pleasure as long as the *person* is right. In other words, there's no such thing as the "wrong" sex, only the wrong person. The sensual woman primarily wants to love and be loved by the whole world.

She will also want as much evidence of her desirability as she can get. Men sometimes want nothing but a vagina into which they can relieve themselves, but a woman seeks much, much more. Today's fully realized woman knows that women are harder to please than men. If you can attract and please another woman, you must be pretty damn good.

8. Bisex Can Be Beautiful; or The ABC's of AC-DC

You might be tempted to skip this chapter—but don't! Bisexuality has its lighter side. As Woody Allen points out, "Bisexuality immediately doubles your chances for a date on Saturday night." Let us therefore look at the other side of the groin, so to speak, in anything but a sober-sided mood.

True bisexuality springs not from sexual promiscuity or sheer sexual need (as among men in prison) but from sexual desire. Allen Drury understood this when, in *Advise and Consent*, he created the character of the happily married Utah senator who once had a homosexual experience. Though he never repeated the act, or even wanted to, he can technically be considered bisexual. Why? Because it was not merely a drunken experience, or one born out of desperate horniness, or something done out of curiosity. An emotional as well as a physical attration motivated him. To me, this is the true test of bisexuality: to need both sexes for more than physical reasons alone.

Bisexuals generate a lot of hostility on both sides of the sexual fence, but not nearly as much as they did five to ten years ago. Homosexuals call them "gay but afraid to admit it." Heterosexuals call them gay, period. Both are wrong. The true bisexual is actually a dual personality, in which the masculine and feminine components alternate with some degree of regularity. Something "comes over" a bisexual, signaling that it's time to seek out a different kind of sex partner.

Unfortunately, bisexual urges create more anxiety in most people than any other sexual manifestation. It's only human to prefer clear-cut, either-or issues; it's easier in many ways to be completely gay or completely straight. This reluctance to stand in the glare of the AC-DC floodlights was revealed in a recent *Forum* magazine survey in which respondents classified themselves according to sexual type. Sixty-three percent of men and seventy-seven percent of women listed themselves as entirely heterosexual; under "some homosexual leanings" were twenty-four percent of men and seventeen percent of women. But only four percent of each sex described themselves as being completely bisexual.

Let me soothe your fears by pointing out some positive aspects of bisexuality:

1. The most obvious characteristic of the bisexual is his or her high libido. When you're hot you're hot, and if you're *really* hot, chances are you're a switch-hitter. This is a commonsense conclusion that doesn't require a degree in psychiatry to figure out, but most people are reluctant to admit it. Low-sexed people seldom get into sexual conflict and are hardly ever anxious, because they *are* low-sexed. The highly sexed person, on the other hand, is forced to shed his or her inhibitions. One sex simply isn't enough, and if you

shed enough inhibitions, you'll eventually "cross over." Bisexuality is, if anything, a bonus and sometimes even a blessing.

2. Men who make the bisexual scene become more tender with women. Once they've experienced the passive role in a homosexual situation, they know "how the other half lives."

3. Women who make the bisexual scene acquire a lustiness and earthiness that men wish all women had. Playing a male role with another woman gives you an exciting touch of ballsiness. I daresay that, without knowing how I got that way, a lot of men admired me for that very quality. We shared the same attitude toward sex, and it gave us a kind of jolly camaraderie.

Female Bisexuality: A Little Help from Your Man

Every woman should be grateful to Erica Jong, author of *Fear of Flying*, for revealing the best-kept female secret in history. We don't always want love, romance, flowers, courting, or any of the other pretty things we're supposed to want. We sometimes want a "zipless fuck," a nameless, faceless stranger whom we'll never see again, just as a man sometimes wants sex with none of the complications of an ongoing affair.

When it comes to female bisexuality, a man who's willing to act as such a sex object can be of vital assistance to two nonlesbian women who want to make it together. The psychological burden of their act is lessened if they can have a man handy to both of them after they've satisfied each other. Real lesbians don't need or want this; heterosexual women who are temporarily into each other do need it. Finishing up with a human "male tool" underscores their essential heterosexuality and keeps them feeling "normal." As they say in every other business, "It's the bottom line that counts."

It's not at all hard to find a man willing to serve in this capacity—most men would crave such a chance. Watching two women make love relieves male homosexual anxiety and helps a man accept his own bisexual longings as well. Besides, it's a great turn-on.

Most men want to join in the fun, and wouldn't mind having intercourse with the dominant woman while she's going down on her lover. Some men like to kiss both women all over. However, if he gets into the act at this point, it's not a true bisexual scene. He should sit there and watch; he can masturbate if he likes, but he shouldn't touch either woman.

When both women have come, he's certain to have one of the finest erections of his life. Now is the time he can enter the game and make love to both women. It doesn't matter which woman he comes in, and it doesn't matter if neither woman comes again. The man's purpose is to "straighten" both women out after they've been gay together, and to complete the bisexual scene. *Bi* means two sexes, and that's what this particular threesome is. If you can get into bisexuality with the aid of a man, you will be better able to accept the whole idea and function without him later on.

Male Bisexuality—With Her Helping Hand

Most women, when asked, will caress a man's anus or insert a finger into it. Men feel that this is all they can rightfully request or expect—but nearly every man wants more.

The average woman doesn't begin to realize how much sexual feeling a man has in his anus. And if she waits for the average man to tell her, she'll very likely wait forever. Men are reluctant to talk about this subject because they fear any mention of it will brand them as homosexuals, either latent or blatant. They will not, for example, tell their woman that they sometimes ejaculate a few drops of semen during a bowl movement, or that they have pleasurable erections during a proctologist's examination. The reasons for these reactions are anatomical and have nothing to do with homosexuality: both the bowel movement and the proctologist run smack into the prostate gland.

The pleasure involved is *sexual* pleasure—not homosexual pleasure or heterosexual pleasure or even bisexual pleasure, but simply pleasure. However, it will probably be a while yet before men can accept this idea without anxiety. And so, until the next book, when I may go into the subject of male homosexuality, which we discussed in the last chapter, and to the ways in which a man can have his bisexual experiences with a woman.

All a woman needs to pleasure a man in a very special bisexual way is a hand equipped with fingers that have carefully trimmed nails. However, you ought to have a rubber glove, not just for the obvious reason but because a lubricated rubber glove stays slippery longer than bare fingers.

This is an act that will give you as much psychological pleasure as it gives him physical pleasure, since it is the most affirmatively aggressive deed a woman can perform in a sexual situation. You can be "male" in this scene as you can never be otherwise, not even if you played the "untouchable butch" in lesbianism. Not only does it give you a release of your own bisexual yearnings, but it also gives you the opportunity to be quite aggressive. Women seldom get such chances—and we all need them occasionally.

This is one time when you should leave his penis alone. Let him masturbate himself, or rub against a pillow. Concentrate on what you're doing and nothing else—*and do it hard!* He will probably ejaculate over the bed, so you might want to put a towel under him.

Warning: Watch out for his testicles; otherwise, it will be a case of killing two stones with one bird.

If you're going to use a dildo on your man, break it to him gently, as you would to a female lover. Don't hold the dildo behind your back and say "Guess what?" and don't go into a long analytical speech beginning, "Everybody has homosexual feelings."

A better approach is to wait until he's been especially virile with you, then whisper to him, "How do you feel about putting out for *me?*" Some men get a thrill out of having the language turned around on them like this.

Another approach is to let him use the dildo on you first. He can masturbate you with it, or he can strap it on and penetrate you with it while he's waiting for his next erection to appear. By the time you've been on the receiving end of it for a few nights, you'll both be used to the idea of a dildo. Your man will then think of it as "our" dildo rather than yours.

Seven out of ten men—my estimate, based on extensive personal research—enjoy being on the receiving end of a dildo as long as a woman does the giving. Make sure your dildo is an average one; the standard six-incher will do nicely; never mind the fourteen-inch "killer" model. I can't say it, and you can't do it, enough—*lubricate!* Put your man on a pile of pillows and climb aboard. Enter him the way you like him to enter you, whether your vagina or your rectum. Ease it in slowly, wait, follow any instructions he gives you, and gradually build up your pumping tempo.

A special thrill is a dildo that ejaculates. Some models have a bulb that can be squeezed, shooting out warm water or milk placed in the imitation testicles. When your man ejaculates, you can have a pseudo-ejaculation of your own. (You'll probably have a real orgasm, too, because the base of the dildo fits up against your clitoris.)

A Wolf in Muff's Clothing

A little pseudo-bisexuality can go a long way. There are scads of in-betweeners—people who are titillated and tempted by the notion of bisexuality but just can't bring themselves to clamber into bed with a member of the same sex. A bit of bisexual playacting by a member of the opposite sex can at least partially satisfy their longings, and even, perhaps, lead them by easy stages to the real thing.

I've told you earlier in this chapter how a woman can play a pseudo-male role with a man. The reverse type of playacting is not as easy, but it can be done. What I *don't* advocate is having a man put on a woman's nightie or perform some other kind of transvestite act. This would turn me off quicker than a faucet, and that applies to every other woman I know.

The child, they say, is father to the man. Some boys, I'm told, occasionally put on an act with their playmates in which they tuck their penis between their tightly closed legs, giving the appearance of a female crotch. Of course, they do this strictly as a gag, but you and I know that behind this byplay there is bi-play—that is, they are unconsciously acting out the role of a girl.

If a man selects a moment before he becomes hard—or after he ceases being hard—he can perform this trick very easily. If he then mounts the woman, or vice versa, or acts out any of the other lesbian positions suggested in this textbook of lovemaking, the simulation of a girl-meets-girl act of intercourse can be quite realistic.

Of course, what will happen is that, partly because of sheer friction but equally as a result of catering to the man's latent homosexual fancies, his penis will revolt, throw off its subservient role, and assert itself in all its manly stature. What is one to do in such a case? Why, let nature take its course—of course! And so you'll both get the best of all possible worlds—bi and hetero.

Back in the 1940s, Dr. Alfred C. Kinsey published the first of his famous reports on American sexual behavior. Perhaps his most controversial finding stemmed from his zero-to-six scale of homosexuality. Those who had never had a gay experience or yearning were classed in zero; those who were exclusively homosexual all their lives were sixes. Everyone else was, therefore, in some way bisexual.

Even in Kinsey's day, the twos, threes, fours, and fives far outnumbered the zeros and sixes. I don't have an exact statistic for the seventies, but you and I both know, beyond any reasonable doubt, that the zeros and sixes among us have dwindled to a precious few. I'm not talking about practicing bisexuals only but also those who have taken an occasional fling or have distinct yearnings in that direction.

The increased interest in bisexuality can be traced in part to several recent developments: the unisex fashion fad; the androgynous appearance of many rock stars; and the motto of the sexual revolution: "If it feels good, do it, as long as it doesn't hurt anybody else."

I would add: "As long as it doesn't hurt *you*." Sometimes we worry so much about the imaginary person called "anybody else" that we forget to worry about number one. If you feel that *you're* ready for it, do it; there are plenty of "anybody elses" out there waiting for you. Then, if it feels good and you keep your head together, keep doing it. But if you don't feel you're ready, wait until you are—even if it turns out to be never.

9. Hey There, Orgy Girl; or A Bicycle Built for Three or More

I've written so much about orgies and swinging parties in my other books that you probably thought there was nothing more to say on the subject. I thought so too, until recently. Well, we're both wrong. Until now I've related my own personal experiences with group sex. As I said in the Introduction, in this book I'm not going to tell you what I've done but what I've learned from having done it.

The difference between the swing and the old-fashioned, garden-variety orgy is like the difference between a Rolls-Royce and a Bentley—more a matter of style than substance. But in sex as in life, that thin line of style can be all that separates total joy from total boredom. So, hang up your hang-ups in the closet, hang loose, and get into the swing of the seventies.

Readers of my other books often write me and ask: "How do you get a swing going? You've told us what happens *during*, but it's the *before* that baffles me."

My answer to this is: nearly everyone has been in on a group swing of some sort or other, so you've already wet your toes in the orgy ocean. It may not have been an orgy by any stretch of the imagination, but even the "indirect" presence of one or more additional persons begins to lean toward that point of the compass. "Open sex" generally begins around age sixteen on a double date, when one guy is driving and the other couple is in the back seat. At some point in the evening, both couples neck and pet in each other's presence, and even if nobody actually goes the limit, it's still a group-sex scene.

Other common experiences include two couples making love in the grass on opposite sides of the car. The car is supposed to be a curtain between them, but they can still hear each other—or even peek under the car between the wheels. Even if everybody gets dressed before they rejoin each other, this moment of reunion still has orgiastic overtones; a certain intimacy springs up between the girl and the *other* boy and the boy and the *other* girl. They didn't make it with each other, but they did the next most intimate thing—they were near each other when it occurred.

The same thing happens when two or more couples have sex in separate rooms of flimsily built beach or ski cottages. The most intimate of these "simulated" group-sex situations, what we can call a near-thing swing, is when two couples share a motel room containing two double beds.

These are all natural situations. My answer to the question "How do you get a swing started?" is: "Let it happen naturally." Otherwise, it's likely to be more embarrassing than titillating.

Believe it or not, this is almost as easily done as said, provided men understand female psychology. It's usually not hard to get men to swing, because men are game for almost anything. The problem

is convincing the women. Well, women are more
easily convinced than you might think.

Your ace in the hole is a competitive spirit
among women. Many women get a kick out of letting other women know how highly sexed they
are. This is the reason behind the mass confes-
sional known as "girl talk"; these no-holds-barred
sessions are *verbal* orgies, and you can bet your
life that women get turned on by them.

In the mock group scenes I've described, women
often pretend more modesty than they actually
feel. At such times, a woman may whisper in
"shocked" tones: "Shh! They'll hear us!" But she
may also get a certain amount of pleasure from
having the other woman realize what's going on.
Women are sexually competitive, too. Listening to
a girlfriend's panting and moaning stimulates her
and is likely to inspire a few sounds of her own;
it's a challenge, because she can't let her girlfriend
outdo her.

Making love in the same room with another
couple is something that most women secretly
crave. Not only is it a challenge to the female ego,
it's an opportunity for two women to liberate each
other with abandoned sexual behavior. If one
woman groans, you can be sure the other will
groan louder.

A swing is much more likely to happen
naturally if the men can persuade the women to
take part in relatively innocent situations such as
the ones I've described. Once the competitive
spirit is unleashed, things are under way. The
most important ingredients of a swing are psychological: it's not so much an opportunity to acquire
new sex partners as an opportunity to indulge in

the two most natural sexual "perversions." These are *voyeurism*, a wish to watch other couples having sex, and *exhibitionism*, a wish to perform before an audience. A third so-called perversion that is also operative is *écouteurism*, from the French word for "listen." The sounds of sex can be the biggest turn-on of all.

Breaking It Gently

When you are with people who are new to swinging, it will get you nowhere to say, "Hey, let's change partners!" Your friends will probably leave as fast as if you had yelled fire.

It's much better to start out with four people, two couples, sharing a motel room. Most women will pretend to be reluctant to share a room with another couple, so the best way to manage this is to save it for a vacation trip. When you and your buddy come back to the car after registering, fib and say that the motel is full up and has only one room. The women will promptly say "Oooh, I just couldn't!"—but they could.

You can even promise that there will be no monkey business. You're just sharing the room to get a good night's sleep. Then tomorrow you'll move on to another motel, where you can have separate rooms. Don't worry. A good night's sleep, hah! The excitement of being aware of another couple in the bed four feet away will soon take over. First one or both of the couples will quietly get in a caress or two. Then certain sounds and whispers will be heard. Then—bingo!

A Hair Away from Lesbianism

In a true swing, the men should have sex with all the women, and the women should all do each other. But inviting two women to go down on each other is too blunt an approach. Again, the rule is, ease them into it with something relatively "innocent" and more or less heterosexual.

Here's a favorite threesome game of mine. The fourth hand is dummy for starters, but it's still a Bob-and-Carol-and-Ted-and-Alice game.

Bob stands behind Alice and thrusts his penis between her thighs. Carol kneels or sits on a chair and sucks the tip of Bob's penis—and, unavoidably, kisses a vagina in the process. Ted stands by, holding his own for the time being.

Once you get as far as this, changing partners will come as naturally as it does on the dance floor.

After the First Ball

Once you've switched partners, you can enjoy some really advanced swing practices. If one or both women are into anal intercourse, you and your buddy can play "Loch Lomond." One of you takes the high road and the other the low road—at the same time.

One man lies on his back; the woman straddles him and takes his penis in her vagina. She leans forward on her knees and braces herself with her palms so that she is upended. The other man kneels behind her and penetrates her rectum.

This is especially stimulating for the men, because the layer of flesh that separates the vagina from the rectum is very thin; the two penises can feel each other through it—a homosexual experience for men who don't want a homosexual experience.

If the other woman feels left out—well, she needn't. She can kneel over the supine man's face; he can kiss her clitoris or her anus, or both, and of course the hard-working girl who's playing the bagpipes can suck her friend's nipples. (I suppose we might as well call this the Highland Swing. And don't say Xaviera doesn't show you some interesting folk dances!)

Tying One On

Here is a "restful" game two couples can play if the women don't feel like having sex right away. The men stand face-to-face with their erect penises side by side and lightly tied together. The women take turns masturbating this bundle until one of the men comes. Whoever comes first gets the woman who was "on duty" when it happened.

Yours, Mine, or Moby's?

You can have a whale of a good time with two women and one dick. This is a fun trick for a threesome, or something to do at a foursome when one of the men needs action and the other is resting.

The man lies down on his back and the two women perform fellatio—simultaneously. Naturally, the girls can't avoid "kissing" each other at the same time they're performing double fellatio—but that's really not so shocking at this point, is it?

Beware the "Talking Swing"

There are lots of people who get off just talking about swinging but who do little or nothing about it. I once picked up a gorgeous couple and invited them to an orgy of mine. In the restaurant where I met them, they were as hang-loose as you could please, but when they came to my apartment they went into a schmaltzy love scene in my bathroom, with everything but singing violins. I heard this passionate moan, then: "Martin, I love you insanely!" This was followed by: "Gloria, I adore you, you're really fantastic!"

As things turned out, they made it only with each other—with their clothes on. These party-poopers got their kicks out of the party, but they took a lot of the kick out of the party, too.

A Place Where Two's Quite a Crowd

Would you believe two penises in one vagina? It works, because I've done it. I once made it simultaneously with two brothers who were inseparable, though I hasten to add not Siamese twins. Like the Tarleton twins in *Gone with the Wind*, they liked to date the same girl and go everywhere together; they even worked in the same office. I suppose there was some sort of latent incestuous homosexuality between them, but judging from their tandem performance with me, they dug women. I sat on top of one while the other circled his brother's hips with his legs and scooted under me. We did it again with me bending over the edge of the bed and the two musketeers kneeling behind my widespread thighs.

The first position was better, but both worked. Although I was too surprised at this doubleheader to climax, it was an experience I wouldn't have wanted to miss. One is company, two's a crowd, and my vagina felt like the subway at rush hour—jam-packed. But it got the passengers where they wanted to go.

The Charity Ball

Some people, mostly women, are so uncomfortable at swings that they look like a "Save This Child" poster. Ironically, this mournful attitude will make some softhearted men have sex with them out of politeness, just as softhearted men in the past would ask the wallflower to dance. Receiving such a charitable contribution from someone who feels sorry for you is an excellent way to destroy your ego. If swings make you this uncomfortable, don't force yourself to participate. No matter what your partner says, no matter how much he or she begs, pleads, or threatens, don't go! It's much easier to find a new lover than to find a new ego.

Along this same line, make sure you look your best before attending a swing. If you are overweight, slim down. We're never so self-aware as when we're in a room full of naked people; what looks all right in your bathroom mirror or with one lover can look entirely different in a crowd.

The most important thing to take into consideration when you decide to swing is the possibility of jealousy between you and your lover. A good way to avoid this is to swing with an acquaintance rather than a lover.

Whether or not you make the group scene is a choice only you can make. The best general advice I can offer comes from Ernest Hemingway: "Right is something I feel good about afterwards; wrong is something that leaves me feeling bad."

10. The Complete Crotch — Hers

Thanks to a puritan heritage, *one* thing a woman never had to worry about in days, or rather nights, gone by was the appearance of her crotch. It was actually more of a case of nonappearance. Fashions always hid it, even in the most licentious periods of history. And when the hoop skirt came along, the protective "bodyguard" was complete. Little boys didn't even know women had *legs*.

In Victorian times, many husbands never saw their wives' genitals because nightgowns were thoughtfully provided with a "connubial aperture"—so that a lady could remain covered from neck to foot without foregoing "connubial bliss."

In the daytime, things were even more discouraging. The average woman wore three petticoats, a crinoline, bloomers, corset cover, corset, and heavy lisle stockings held up by buckram straps. What man could cope with all these protective layers? Besides, he might get arrested for murder: tossing a woman's skirts up in those days could easily result in suffocation. Men had to go to so much trouble to get at a vagina that they were content simply to know it was *there*. It would never have occurred to them to try to scrutinize it. As the nineteenth century Harvard Medical

School professor told his class: "Gentlemen, today we will discuss something none of you has ever seen—the female genitalia."

Thanks to this situation, women of the past were blissfully free of concern about the most female part of themselves. All that has changed now; frontal nudity in movies and magazines, nude bathing, nude lovemaking, and superintimacies in the bedroom have made women equal to men in a way that's not altogether advantageous. They must now concern themselves about what's between their legs.

What are some of the crotch dilemmas women now have?

Matching the Snatch

When Benjamin Franklin said "all cats are gray at night," he was using "cat" the way we use "pussy." In his day, when people saved sex for the dark of night, all but the blondest pubic hair did look like a chocolate swirl.

An old saying favored by men has long been: "There's one way to tell if she's a natural blond." It's not true. Except for near-albino Scandinavian types, blond women generally have brownish pubic hair. A golden blond's thatch is more sandy or buff; women with dark-blond or "dirty-blond" hair usually have dark-brown pubic hair that doesn't reveal its burnished glint unless it's directly under a light. Women with light brown or darker hair on the head will be definitely brunette down below.

Among these fair women, anything can happen between the legs. I knew a girl with sandy-blond hair on her head whose pubic hair was a two-toned mixture of no-color buff with a few strands of contrasting chestnut here and there. Some very blond people, both males and females, are what might be called "social" blonds who are really genetic redheads. You've seen blond men whose mustaches and beards come out red? Well, it's the same way with women of this type: their love bushes are ruddy. (Blonds of this sort usually have a lot of freckles, too, so that's another way to tell an underground redhead without taking off her clothes.)

There's no such thing as an exact match, and no such thing as a golden-blond crotch growth, despite the repeated use of this description in porno novels. Even if it started out golden, it would soon be darkened by time and lack of exposure to the light.

True brunettes are the only ones that match up top and bottom. Strawberry blonds come closer to matching, but "brunette redheads"—the coppery auburn types—are generally an ordinary darkish brown or sometimes reddish brown in the pelvis.

Natural blonds who are dark in the crotch often worry that men will think they bleach their head hair when they really don't. Such women needn't worry at all; many men have told me that a darker bush on a natural blond is more exciting than a total match. One man I know says that too-blond pubic hair makes him feel like a pedophil-iac. A woman with light crotch hair reminds him of a little girl, whereas a darker swatch is more adult somehow, and hence sexier. (At least, as far as *that* man is concerned; it could turn some men on.) Generally, I think men enjoy a contrast between top and bottom hair because it makes for complexity, and complex women are more interesting than those who are too much "all of a piece."

Black-haired women worry about their pubic hair being too dark. Actually, they're not as dark as they seem. Brunettes are usually hairier than blonds, and the abundance makes the hair look darker than it really is. Trim the hair short, and it will seem at least one shade lighter, if that's what you want.

Some redheaded women worry about having a strange-looking crotch. These are the women who have brick or carrot-red hair and pinkish pubic hair. They needn't worry; better to take advantage of the surprise element they have to offer to men who have never seen a shade like that before. Men tend to find pinkish love hair very winsome, so there's no cause for worry.

Should you dye Little Eva's curls? Frankly, I can't imagine why anyone would want to, unless you're a jet-black brunette who's bleached her head out to near-white and have suddenly decided to take up skinny-dipping in the Central Park lagoon on Sunday afternoon. If that's the case, you'll soon have much more to worry about than your crazy-mixed-up hair.

There are some avant-garde hairdressers who dye pubic hair, though how they get that little rubber cap on, I'm sure I don't know.

Bushwhacker's Delight

Henry Miller claimed that a shaved pelvis looks like a dead clam. Most men, I've found, are delighted with a nice hairy snatch on a woman. There's a town in England called Bushy, the very mention of which makes men grin with delight; the countless jokes that have grown up around this place are testimony to what men really like between a woman's legs. ("You have to go through Bushy first to get to where you're going," for example.)

I think what charms men about women's pubic hair is the "something-in-common" element; a woman is smooth all over, yet in that one place she's like a man. Thus, it may be that everyone's bisexuality is stirred by the idea of this thick patch of hair on a woman's body. Alternatively, the fascination may lie in the fact that hairiness suggests animality, which in turn suggests unbridled sex. Whatever it is, *everybody* is very fond of—and very proud of—the famous fuzzy triangle.

However, human nature is contrary; now that crotches are out in the open, the question "to shave or not to shave" has swept the country, as the many letters I receive testify. (You have no idea how many letters I get every day on every imaginable subject—some of them not even dealing with sex.)

Much of the shaving controversy is due to simple curiosity. Even men who claim they love to plow through a real bramble bush sometimes want to see what their woman's crotch looks like bare, and may ask her to shave it just so they can have a look. Women are also curious about themselves. Long before the shaving controversy came out in the open, just about every woman shaved herself once to see what it would look like. Some women were shocked; they claimed that lack of hair made them feel "desexed," as if they had reverted to prepuberty days and had become little girls again. Some were astonished at how *small* their genitals really are—no bigger than an egg; they felt a reduction in their self-esteem and couldn't wait for the hair to grow back again so they'd "feel big down there"—that is, sexually capable. Some women were pleased that they were so small and "dainty."

Generally, I'd say that unless a man who wants you to shave is motivated by a once-for-fun curiosity, he bears watching. A man who likes a woman perpetually clean-shaven may really like her to look defenseless and vulnerable, because there's nothing more fragile-looking than a bald nest egg. Without the hair covering the slit, it looks like one of Mother Nature's unfinished jobs.

Shaving completely also results in practical difficulties. If you're easily excited, being bald down there can be quite distracting. The rub of silky panties is too much sometimes; it's a nice game for a "oneplay" mood when you deliberately want to savor self-stimulation (a subject I'll get to in a later chapter), but not so good on a daily basis, when you're called upon to concentrate on other things, like work. Nor should you forget the torments of "barber's itch."

Personally, I don't choose to shave, nor do I like

to go down on a woman who does—I don't want to scrape my mouth against her five-o'clock shadow. However, a *clipped* bush is something else. Every woman I sleep with and I have "the mark of Xaviera." Here's how to qualify:

Unless you're very hairy and/or wear very skimpy bikinis, leave the hair on the lower belly alone, since it doesn't get in the way of anything or anybody. Clip the hair on the sides of the vulva so that it won't get caught in your pants bands and pull. Clip the hair very short, starting at the top of the slit; be especially careful to clip thoroughly around the clitoris so that your lover can get to it with his (or her) tongue.

Pay special attention to the long, straggly hairs underneath. Pull on the longest hairs so that the flesh of the lip is pulled down with them; this gives you a margin of safety so that you'll be able to see what you're doing and not cut yourself.

Having gone down this far, we may as well follow the hairline around to the rear, since it's almost part of the crotch. All women have some hair there, but a few have a nice, big fuzzy crescent of it, and it turns me on something terrific. Many men have agreed with me, and one customer at my house in New York specifically asked for a girl who was especially well-endowed in this area.

If you feel that you have too much for either visual aesthetics or good daily hygiene, you can cut it—provided you're double-jointed. A sexier solution is to ask your lover to cut it for you with a pair of *blunt-tipped* mustache scissors. If he has a mustache, he'll be able to provide the scissors, and if he *really* loves you, he'll be willing to share them with you.

Accidentally-on-Purpose Department

Some women like to leave their crotch hair completely alone in order to tease with it. Letting a few strands "accidentally" escape from their bikinis is one way. Personally, I think this is a turn-off in a bathing suit but a turn-on in underpants. But these things, as I say, are personal. Some people may react in the opposite way, and probably a lot of men would be turned on by a peek at a few strands of crotch hair no matter when they saw it.

The nostalgia craze has recently brought back the boxer-style underpants, called step-ins, that women wore in the thirties. Some women have switched to them because they tend to "girt"—i.e., the crotch seam bisects the vagina, so that the lips are divided. Worn under a snug pair of slacks or jeans, boxer-style panties have enabled men to become crotch-watchers, too. Worn under a skirt, they give a man something to look up to when the woman is on a balcony or a flight of stairs. Again, I'd say that letting *everybody* see your "better halves" is a little much, but I feel very sexy when *one* man sees me in the panties alone.

(*Caution:* Boxer panties can drive you crazy until you get used to them. You'll "pull at your pants" in public like a twelve-year-old boy. When they really start riding up on you, it's like sitting on a scythe.)

Looking for Ms. Goodbush

Men who like big bushes can test for them beforehand. Look at a woman's forearms, the backs of her hands, her first finger joints, her eyebrows, and her toes. If she's hairier than average in these places, she will very likely be hairy where you want her to be hairy.

A woman's coloring does *not* indicate the extent of her hairiness. The so-called "Irish brunette" with jet-black hair and pale skin often has virtually hairless arms and legs and a sparse, neatly triangled but very blue-black pubic growth. There's a blond type, on the other hand, that I call the "Sicilian WASP," who is blond on the head but who has nearly black hair, and lots of it, elsewhere.

Something that a lot of men consider a real find is the woman with a hairline running from the bottom of the navel into the stomach growth. Men make up statistics as they go along. Whatever they find on a woman, they will praise to the skies—at least, to her face—and claim that they *love* it. A woman I know who has such a hairline tells me that several of the men she's slept with have assured her that many of the women they've bedded have a hairline on their stomachs.

I don't know how many "many" is, but I do believe men are telling the truth when they say they like hairlines. Again, it's something calculated to excite both a man's and a woman's natural bisexuality. I also possess a thin hairline, and I've seen plenty of them and find them a turn-on; it makes a woman seem a little like a man—kind of natural, earthy, and sex-loving. And as Rex Harrison once sang so plaintively, "Why can't a woman be more like a man?"

Loose Lips

Some women have saggy outer lips that look like tiny hair-covered testicles. Contrary to general opinion, this is not caused by too much childbirth; I've seen it in women who have never even been pregnant. If they were men, they would probably have big, loose scrotal sacks, since the areas are analogous.

In the days when masturbation was said to cause blindness and insanity in men, loose lips on a woman were a sign that she "pulled on herself." A few women do masturbate this way, because tugging on the outer lips exerts rhythmic tugging on the clitoris, but the number of women who use this masturbatory technique is very small. (I've never known one.) There's no discernible cause for sagging lips except heredity. They are *not* caused by having too much sex—if they were, I'd have tripped over mine years ago. (If you have saggy lips—but only if this condition really bothers you—see a reputable plastic surgeon; it won't cost you as much as a nose job, and it will help much more in the clutch.)

There is one type of woman who is almost certain to have saggy lips—the butch lesbian or bull dyke, also called a bull dagger, who likes to pee standing up. I saw a "girl" do this once, and I couldn't believe my eyes. It was in a lesbian bar, and she made bets with everyone present that she could do it.

Here's how I lost ten dollars. She stood in front of the john, dropped her pants, and pulled her lips into a long spout, She had been peeing like this since she was twelve, she said, and I believed it; she had a good five inches of lip when she stretched it out. Sure enough, the stream hit the back of the bowl, exactly like a man's. Just before she packed it all back into her pants, I got a look at it. Her lips were like deflated balloons. Only a Ubangi could have loved them.

The Holland Tunnel

So much has been said about the size of the penis that it was to be expected that, with today's new frankness, the size of the vagina would also be considered openly. Men are also in a turn-about-is-fair-play mood on this subject, and that was to be expected, too. Since women want to be equal, some men are now saying, "All right, let them be equal—let them worry about size as we've done all along"—quite forgetting that we have *always* worried ourselves silly about breast size. Unfortunately, these same men are now saying things like, "The tighter the saddle, the better the ride," to counter the female saying, "The bigger the instrument, the sweeter the music."

Again, the size of a woman's vagina has nothing to do with the number of children she's had or the number of men she's bedded down with. In *The Godfather*, the woman who couldn't satisfy a man until she met hung-like-an-ox Sonny Corleone had *always* been big, and she'd never had any children. Extreme cases such as this are correctable with surgery.

For less extreme cases, there are home remedies that will make you temporarily tighter. For centuries, women whose husbands have been away a long time have had to think of some way to be nice and snug when their men returned, so that hubby would have no reason to suspect they'd been cheating. Women who have not had sex for a long time tend to shrink up, some even becoming nearly as tight as virgins. Men who are used to one woman can often tell the difference, so if you cheat while he's away, you can repair the damage with vinegar or lemon douches. Don't use too much vinegar, though, or he'll think you've been making it with a dill pickle. In Florence King's recent book, *Southern Ladies and Gentlemen*, a "perpetual virgin" at the University of Mississippi is described as douching with Lavoris for every date—so that he would find her in a state of "pucker power."

The Jolly Pink Giant Clitoris

I don't know how this could be a problem, because it sounds like a blessing to me. I think a big clitoris is sexy, but some women feel that if it protrudes visibly between the lips, it is somehow masculinizing. Actually, nearly every man I've ever talked to is thrilled by the sight of an obviously excited and erect "trigger."

Having, I hope, successfully demolished the various myths about the aesthetics of the female genitalia, I'd like to turn to the male apparatus in the next chapter. There's nothing ugly about our sex organs. It's only that centuries of repression and puritanical nonsense have given many of us ugly *thoughts* about them. Get rid of these false notions, and you'll soon start enjoying the beauty of *all* parts of the human body, both yours and your partner's.

11. The Complete Crotch — His

Even in this cocksure age, many men still think their genitals are ugly or repulsive to women—that while women may love the way a penis feels, they aren't crazy about how it looks.

As cock-and-bull stories go, this one isn't hard to figure out. A subconscious reason for this attitude is the resemblance of the penis to the snake, that eternal symbol of evil hated by everyone. "A snake in his pants" is a revealing (and insulting) name for the male organ.

The penis has been burdened with countless ridiculous and mocking nicknames. How can you possibly have any respect or affection for something called a "dingus," "dingle," "dangle," "dooly," "pee-pee," "dong," "schlong," "schmuck," "putz," or "dead-eye dick"? Even "prick" suggests something relatively harmless and trivial. A *pin* pricks.

While it's true that women's genitals have unfortunate nicknames, too, there's an important difference between the way these names are used. Women never—well, almost never—hurl genital expletives at one another; but men, on the other hand, make a practice of calling one another such names as "prick," "schmuck," or "putz."

Still another "penile-image" issue is what issues from the organ. The penis squirts or dribbles a substance that most men find unappetizing to contemplate. This is probably a carryover from the messy business of coping with the stuff on their hands or clothing during youthful masturbation sessions.

"Making a mess" is an exclusively male problem; regardless of all the other problems women have to cope with, there's no comparable sexual mess-making in the female world. Even menstrual discharges can't compare to ejaculation in this regard. An ejaculation can occur anytime, with little or no advance warning, whereas menstruation, bothersome though it is, can at least be *timed* and therefore *confined*. But who ever heard of an ejaculation napkin? The male of the species must cope as best he can. No wonder so many mothers wonder why in the world their adolescent sons keep "losing" all those pocket handkerchiefs.

When a Fellatio Needs a Friend

Proof that men find their own semen unpleasant is not hard to find. A standard male fantasy that psychiatrists report, especially prevalent in men who are hostile to women, is the fantasy of forced fellatio. In this fantasy, the man always "makes her swallow it." If she has to be *made* to do this, then it must be a horrible experience, right?

Men have always been reluctant to ask their wives to perform fellatio. Even now, many men still believe that "decent" women shouldn't or won't do it, and so they go to a prostitute for their fellatio. When I was a hooker and later a madam, countless men came to me for fellatio, explaining that they couldn't very well ask their wives to do it. Of course, many of them would have been pleasantly surprised had they summoned the courage to make the suggestion. But I didn't tip them off in those days. It would have been bad business.

X-rated movies provide another, less obvious clue that men unconsciously dislike their penises. Cunnilingus scenes are few and far between, and the male actors do not praise the taste, juiciness, or appearance of the vulva. But fellatio happens every few minutes, and the "actresses" go into ecstasies about how beautiful and tasty the penis is, and how much they love to swallow come. "Oh, it tastes *sooo* good!" This would seem to disprove the theory, but remember that these scenes are written, directed, and filmed by and for men. In trying to reassure themselves that the penis is indeed an object of beauty, they "protest too much."

Women's reaction to exhibitionists has bolstered men in their belief that the penis is a frightening and disgusting sight. Naturally, women, and especially little girls, tend to scream when they come upon a strange man with his fly open. It's not that they are disgusted—just startled and frightened. They don't fear the penis, just the man, and that he might force it upon them against their will.

The male notion that a penis disgusts women leads to a feeling on the part of some men that their whole bodies are disgusting. Up until the early 1940s, men were expected to wear tops to their bathing suits. Earlier in the century, etiquette demanded that no gentleman even permit a lady to see him in his shirt-sleeves. If a woman entered the room, a man had to put on his jacket, no matter what the temperature was. (Some older men still do this automatically.)

In my opinion, the recent streaking fad was men's way of saying in effect: "I'm tired of being thought ugly. Look at me. I'm beautiful, too!" This is a statement the ancient Greek sculptors made over and over again. I think it's wrong to arrest someone for making that statement today just because he makes it in the flesh.

Penile Reform

Here are ways a woman can help change a man's negative self-image:

• Don't avoid looking at a man's penis. Many women do this even today, possibly because of a traumatic experience with an exhibitionist—which so many women have had at some point in their lives, usually when they were children and were warned *not to look*. The warning was so severe (along with all the other warnings they got on the subject of sex) that they grew up averting their eyes from just about everything.

Some women feel that looking directly at their man's penis is voyeuristic leering—and leering is something that only men do. Most men would *love* to be leered at; a good leer among friends never hurt anyone, male or female, and it's a gesture of appreciation as much as anything else.

• Don't studiously ignore the situation while a man is putting on a rubber, French tickler, penis ring, or whatever. Instead, offer to put it on for him. Many men have asked me why women show mild distaste when a man is applying a rubber to his penis. The answer is simple and not at all insulting: it reminds her of a gynecologist putting on his rubber glove and preparing to insert a cold metal speculum in her vagina. The association with clinical procedures would naturally change her mood for a moment, but it has nothing to do with her feelings about you. No offense intended.

• Do not—repeat, do not—ask a man to use a condom when you give him head. You can't get pregnant through the mouth, so it's an insult rather than a precaution. Remember, penises have feelings, too.

• If you don't care to swallow his come, don't—but don't spit it out in his sight, and don't run into the bathroom to get rid of it in the toilet. The sound of a toilet flushing afterward—and women are the world's greatest toilet-flushers; *any* reason will do—will cause a man to make unflattering associations about his semen, which has been rejected like so much body waste.

Personally, I don't always like the taste of semen. I get rid of it in a towel or in a tissue I have already planted under the mattress or in some other place I can easily reach. Always have a large bottle of mouthwash handy in the bathroom.

If a man still thinks that semen tastes like whipped cream, swallow half of the semen, then quickly come up and give him a deep tongue kiss, while you simultaneously deposit the other half of his sperm in his mouth. The majority of men will jump up and immediately spit it out and rinse their mouths.

• Pat your man's penis during nonsexual moments. Give it a pet name such as "John Thomas," used by Lawrence's Lady Chatterley; or name it after its owner, calling it "Junior"—"David, Junior," "Mark, Junior," etc. A girl I know has long, hilarious conversations with someone named Penis Desmond—P.D., for short—who answers her in a high-pitched falsetto voice. This little act is a fun way to humanize a woman's relationship to a man's penis.

• Use more than your hands to caress your man's penis. If you have long hair, wrap it around his shaft and pull it captive, close to your face, then kiss the tip and murmur sweet nothings to it. It won't be long before it answers you back in the nicest possible way.

The Big P

I wrote in *The Best Part of a Man* that if I had been a man, I would want the biggest penis possible, even though I know—probably better than anyone else—that sheer size isn't all that important. However, I *don't* think I would measure it down to the last millimeter like the many men who write me about their size worries.

For example, this is one short silly sentence excerpted from a long silly letter: "My cock is 5 4/9″ long when erect and 3 2/7″ when soft; is that all right?"

They say women are better at details than men, but I wonder. If I were a man, I would round my penis measurement off to the nearest inch—although I must admit it would be the nearest even inch *above*—but I would *not* fritter away my time with all these fractions. Incidentally, I have no idea where men find such accurate tape measures.

Women, with the best intentions, can add to a man's fears about inadequate size. Nearly every woman protests too vigorously and too quickly: "Size doesn't matter, it's what you do with it . . ."

This is true—to a point. Size *does* matter if it's so tiny that she can't even feel it, or if it slips out the moment she starts to wriggle. Fortunately, few penises are this small.

Size also matters when a woman is with a man purely for sex with no love or affection involved. At times like this, she want a big one. With a man she cares about and has a real relationship with, the *whole* man is more important than the sum of his parts.

The *kind* of size matters to a woman, too. Men worry mainly about length, whereas women care more for girth. As far as length goes, it can go too far—literally a "big bang" in the most uncomfortable way. As the old saying goes: "More than enough is a waste"—meaning that if he's all the way in, up against her cervix, yet there are still two inches on the outside, these are two useless inches.

Girth is another matter. Being thick-headed isn't so bad—as long as you're thick-headed only below the waist. A penis is hardly ever too thick. Women like a "fisty" approach.

Big Ones vs. Huge Ones

A bonus is always nice, but there's nothing to do with a yardstick except measure for new draperies. I got a letter from a man who assured me that the problems of small men were nothing compared to *his*. His penis measured twelve inches soft and fifteen hard, and he was a twenty-six-year-old virgin.

Some women dream of a penis like this, but that's all they do. The "telephone pole" is another female fantasy, but most don't want to get any closer than fantasy. My correspondent told me that women pursued him when word got around about how he was built, but that all they wanted to do was look at it. Some wanted to touch it— quickly, like a hot stove—and a few brave ones wanted to suck it. But even that was a problem for him, because it had a head like a baseball; his girth was 5½ inches. Naturally, no woman could give him a real deep-throat job without risking her life, and some couldn't even get his head into their mouths.

The poor fellow tried to solve his problem, or at least remedy it, by buying an artificial vagina—

but he split it up the middle the first time he used it. And there was no warranty.

The only thing to do with such an endowment is try to insert it in a vagina when it's soft, making sure that the man wears a penis guard that will stop him from thrusting too far. A woman who is banged in her ovary experiences the same pain as a man who gets kicked in the balls.

Life's Little Ironies

To me, the only time a penis looks funny is when it doesn't fit its owner. A beautiful big erection on a small man, for instance. This is even stranger-looking than a tiny penis on a big stocky man. Both will probably feel good when they are put where they belong, but the first time a woman sees them is a jarring experience. The little squirt with the big squirter is a very prevalent type, which is just one reason why men's penile size should not be judged by their outward physical build and height. When the little squirt kibitzes behind you at a poker game, you know he's there.

Clippies vs. Trumpets

The circumcision controversy is rearing its ugly/pretty head. (Choose one.) According to a recent survey by a sex magazine, the number of women preferring an uncircumcised penis and the number preferring a circumcised one canceled each other out. It was fifty percent for the one and fifty percent for the other—as far as intercourse was concerned.

Oral sex was another matter. Only eleven percent actually preferred an uncircumcised penis, whereas forty-five percent said they had a strong preference for clipped penises. Their reason was hygiene, not appearance. Apparently the sight of a hanging foreskin in itself does not bother most women; the fact that it *covers up* something does. Concealment is next to uncleanliness in our minds; we tend to think that what is underneath any covering might possibly be dirty—like the rug under which the lazy housekeeper sweeps floor dust.

Yet even women who refuse to go down on an uncircumcised penis say that they love to play with them. There's a child in all of us, and I must admit that a trumpet penis has more movable parts than a clippie. Peeling back the foreskin to see what's underneath is bound to appeal to the child in us. I know one woman who likens the emergence of her lover's unusually large and purplish glans to a jack-in-the-box she remembers from her nursery-school days. This same woman not only enjoys fellatio, but adds something to the act that would be impossible with a clipped penis: she pulls the long foreskin up and out, then inflates it like a balloon. She calls this "playing the trumpet." The air pressure drives her lover out of his head—this time, the one above the waist.

For the woman who likes to give head but doesn't like a man to ejaculate in her mouth, a foreskin can be a convenience. When he is about to come, she can close the foreskin with her fingers and continue to masturbate him until he comes. The warmth of the semen under the hood feels terrific to most men; afterward the woman can release the foreskin and collect the semen in her hand. She might even rub it on her breasts as ancient Chinese women did. This way, she "takes" it, if not exactly in the way he'd expect.

Another advantage of the trumpet penis: it gets more fun out of a hand-job than clippies do. The foreskin is like a built-in penis ring; rolled back to grip tightly around the glans, it creates a pressure that is hard to beat (and easier to beat *off*) for the woman who doesn't know much about hand-jobs.

A caution: when you masturbate a trumpet penis, please remember to remove your rings, especially when you use lubrication. Many rings tend to turn around on the finger, and your two-inch-diameter cocktail ring with the seventeen-pointed star might lose you the best part of a lover.

Some women say that the wrinkly foreskin sets up more vaginal friction during intercourse, but personally, I've never been able to tell the difference. Like the women mentioned in the survey, however, I don't like to go down on a trumpet. Maybe I'm hung up on this subject because I'm half-Jewish—the half that counts—but I think it's simply a matter of aesthetics. Until all unclipped men learn to wash thoroughly under their foreskins, I'll save my oral talents for their shorn brothers.

The Myth of Rationed Ejaculations

A study of history and anthropology reveals a
long-standing but scientifically erroneous association between seminal fluid and strength. Even today, many football coaches forbid their players to
have sex the night before a game for fear it will
drain them of the physical power they need. From
this attitude has grown the.feeling that too much
sex will enervate a man and cause premature impotence. Some men believe they have been sup-
plied a certain number of ejaculations, to be
distributed throughout their lifetime, and that if
they go over this limit they'll find themselves
"burned out" or "drained dry."

This attitude causes many men to resent a
highly sexed woman, even though they may really
crave her aggressiveness and enthusiasm. Conflict
results, and psychological problems, including impotence, are the frequent result.

Not only is there no basis for this "rationing"
belief, but the opposite is true. "Use it or lose it"
is a good rule to follow. This doesn't mean that
you should compulsively go to bed with any
woman; that can cause impotence, too. It merely
means that when mind, emotions, and body all say
"Go!" then for God's sake *go*. But make sure all
three are in working order, or *you* won't work. If
you're truly not attracted to a woman, it's better
to go home and masturbate than to risk the hostility and emptiness that come after a sex act with

someone you simply don't like. The only thing you should ration is compulsiveness.

A Whole New Ball Game

Very few women reach adulthood without acquiring a nervous attitude toward testicles. Some women are scared to death of them. The "ball scare" has kept many women from being good lovers. Very early in life, every girl is given advice on how to "kick a man where it hurts" to protect herself from rapists. A favorite expression that goes with these lectures is "You can cripple him for life." It's not surprising, therefore, that many women avoid testicles like the plague.

To make matters worse, most women have seen or at least heard about men in dire pain from a scrotal injury. Accidents at sports events are common, but even more unavoidable is that childhood contretemps—a little boy falling on a bike bar. This trauma could be easily avoided if only there were no such things as boys' and girls' bikes. I often wonder if the civilized world—if we can call it that—secretly wants to castrate men at an early age. If either sex should have a bike with a bar on it, it ought to be girls. The "boys' bike" with the bar across it is not only unnecessary but a virtual invitation to serious injury. Better that all children ride "girls' bikes."

Despite these associations, there are some women who come through childhood with a healthy attitude toward testicles. After all, balls are equated with guts and courage, and everyone

admires a guy who is "ballsy." Some women are so
fascinated by them that they claim they could tell
their different lovers while blindfolded with just
one fast feel of the *cojones*. Once a woman learns
to accept them as an enjoyable part of her lover's
body, she'll become a knowledgeable umpire.

I know a woman who would rather have a big
set of testicles on a man than a big penis—a situation known as "all potatoes and no meat." She
claims that the feel of her lover's enormous sack
against her anal area during intercourse is the
thing that helps her to orgasm. A man with very
hairy testicles can accidentally tickle his woman's
buttocks in such a way that she moves faster while
they're having sex, and thus help her to come
more quickly and joyfully.

There are visual preferences among ball-happy
women, too. Most of the women I've talked to say
they prefer lots of black hair in this area of a man.
But you don't have to be ball-happy to get a kick
out of them. They come with the territory, and
even if they make you nervous, you're probably
enjoying them without knowing it. Forget about
the ball scare and put the balls back into balling.

Liberated Penis Envy

I disagree with Freudian psychoanalysts who say
that women envy a man his penis. No woman
wants a penis of her own. What in the world
would she do with it? And how many people of either sex would want to sleep with her? Maybe

once, for curiosity's sake, but as a steady arrangement it would get a little weird, to say the least.

The truth of the matter is—and this is what the psychiatrists really mean—that *if* a woman were a man, she would, like me, want the liveliest, biggest, strongest, handsomest penis in the world. In place of that, she wants to *borrow* such a penis from the man she goes to bed with.

One way a woman can enjoy a "borrowed" penis is to perfect the art of unzipping a fly. Imagine that opening a man's pants and taking out his penis is the same as opening a gift. Nothing can equal the special excitement you feel when you unbuckle his belt, lower his zipper, and pull aside the flaps of his shirttail and shorts. Think of the different materials of his clothing as the different wrappings that must be removed from a real gift: first the plain mailing wrapper, then the colored wrapping, then the tissue in which the gift is packed. And *then* the big, beautiful surprise inside!

When you unwrap a penis, do what you would naturally do with a gift. Take it in your hand, hold it up, look at it from various angles, study it as you think about all the places you can put it. It's yours now; the gift has become a possession.

Well, that pretty much unwraps the subject. But for men who want to give women the thrill of a lifetime, buy a pair of Navy-surplus sailor pants with the square-front opening—the kind with thirteen buttons commemorating the original thirteen states. (I'm serious; that's why there are thirteen buttons.) A favorite female fantasy is that of a penis springing suddenly out of a man's pants. A penis will often get caught in narrow verticle flies or twisted in a man's underwear, but a Navy flap-front is like the trick door of a jack-in-the-box. There's nothing like a pop-up penis to surprise and delight the little girl in all of us. I'm Xaviera Hollander, and that's the way it was thirteen buttons ago.

One final note on liberated penis envy: not only is it a healthy female indulgence, but it should also give men a healthier attitude toward their supposedly unlovely genitals. After all, would anyone envy someone an unenviable possession?

12. The Nonstop Joyride; or Unendurable Pleasure Indefinitely Prolonged

Now that you know how to get it on, it's time you learned to *keep* it up—and in. The late Aly Khan, according to numerous reliable accounts, masterfully practiced the art of prolonged coitus without coming. And he, of course, was a Johnny-come-lately. The technique goes back to biblical and pre-biblical days. For example, the ancient Chinese believed in two concepts that their philosophy emphasized—marked prolongation of the act of copulation, and copulation without ejaculation.

More recently, in the nineteenth century, the Oneida Community, a group whose revolutionary experiment in communal living stressed proficiency in the art of lingering almost indefinitely on the borderline of orgasm without splashing over. They made it doubly difficult by also encouraging the free exchange of sexual partners, and as everyone knows, novelty is a strong aphrodisiac.

Dragging it out, as opposed to pulling it out, is something that all men dream of achieving. One reason is simple: it's better for the woman if the man can make sex last as long as possible. But there's also a widespread belief that the sperm is a vital fluid that should be hoarded rather than expended, for the male *allegedly* loses his powers with each loss of sperm. Most men have tried various obvious techniques to hold back ejaculation. The one most practiced, of course, is reciting the multiplication tables, either forward or backward, depending upon which way you're screwing. Of course, if this is overdone, the guy will be left reciting the tables to perfection, oblivious to his penis, which will have gone as limp as overcooked macaroni.

Language buffs like to do Latin declensions. As for literary recitations, they may start silently in your mind, but you may find yourself mumbling aloud. I was once in bed with an Englishman who was reciting Henry V's rallying speech to his troops. Unfortunately, Shakespeare wrote this to end with a patriotic frenzy. When my lover got to "God for Harry, England, and St. George!" he was so stirred that he left me high and dry and my bed soaking wet.

Actually, these popular methods are pretty high-schoolish. The real aficionado strives for a state of complete relaxation and euphoria while still dwelling on the pleasures at hand.

There are much better ways to delay ejaculation. Some are tried and true and have passed into legend; others are based on simple common sense.

Mind over Matter

Men who plan to make a big sexual day—or night—of it are more than likely to do everything wrong. They pick a Saturday or Sunday, which is logical enough considering most employment arrangements. However, since nearly everyone else is also on a five-day week, weekends are phone-ringing, door-ringing time. It's also the time for all sorts of people to come around—salesmen, political workers, and anyone else who would like to find the entire household at home. The result? The moment you're in bed and really going good, the paper boy shows up asking for *his*, too—all $2.50 of it. And pretty soon you'll be asking yourself, "Why is coitus so damned interruptus?"

Another mistake is playing an erotic soundtrack. It may be on LP, but because of its speedy effect on you, you might as well play it at 78. The idea is to *delay* ejaculation, not to speed it up. You want to make one erection last an hour; you don't want to get so excited that you're up and down five times in an hour. That's another art. I'm talking about the long-playing, long-lasting, non-stop erection.

What's good for the goose is good for the gander. Trying to delay ejaculation after you've penetrated a woman is like to trying to avoid drowning after you've gone down for the third time. It's simply too late.

Most men penetrate as deeply as possible on the first thrust, and then expect—somehow—to hold back. Once a penis has met head-on with a cervix, there's no place for it to go except *off*.

Since quick orgasm is an exclusively male problem, avoid it by pretending that you aren't male. Be a tease instead; forget about total penetration and adopt the characteristics of the coy sixteen-year-old female virgin. Do all the things she would do: be bold, then be frightened; go forward, then retreat; be capricious, indecisive, and *seemingly* unsure of whether you actually intend to go through with it or not.

When you climb between your woman's legs, don't penetrate her vagina. Instead, separate the outer lips with your penis and rub it up and down from clitoris to vagina, and farther down to her anus. Then insert the head of your penis until it's just inside the vaginal vestibule. When your lover feels this, she'll rise up to meet you and pull you in. *Don't let her.* Tease her instead by pulling out entirely.

Do this several times, as many times as necessary to give you a feeling of control. The more you tease in this manner, the more desperate for *all* of your penis your woman will become. She'll become overeager, impatient, and hurried, whereas you, by contrast, will enact the role of the cool partner.

When you're both ready to perish from all this teasing, enter her—*but don't begin thrusting*. Instead, leave it there without moving at all—and without letting her move.

Instead of the old in-and-out, make rocking, swaying motions with your body while keeping your penis completely still. Then begin to pull back, but do it very slowly, so slowly that she barely feels it. When the tip of your penis is nearly out of her vagina, give another hard thrust forward and repeat the process—that is, leave it in and resume the rocking and swaying.

By now, your lover will be fully aroused. This will make you feel even more controlled, because the more frenzied a woman becomes, the more confidence a man feels in his own patience and serenity. If you begin to feel close to a climax at any stage of the teasing process, pull out entirely and rest your penis lightly between her cheeks or against her stomach. If she makes clutching, writhing motions, take it away from her entirely until she's still.

Carezza, the Ultimate Fantasy

Carezza means "caress" in Italian. It's a more appealing word for what used to be called, with all the romance of a pharmaceutical prescription, "male continence." "Continence" sounds too much like "abstinence" to be palatable, but actually they're two different words and worlds. "Continence" means "to contain," and "abstinence" means "to refrain entirely." The continence in *carezza* does not refer to the containment of sexual encounters, but to the containment or control of the male orgasm in *each* encounter.

Practitioners of *carezza* have sex as often as they wish, but ideally the male refrains from ejaculation unless a pregnancy is desired. Are you ready to explode just from thinking about such a thing? Actually, it's not nearly so bad as it sounds; in fact, devotees of the art claim it's heaven on earth.

This brings us back to square one, the Oneida Community. *Carezza* got its start in the 1840s at Oneida, the upper New York State communal experiment, an early version of today's communes. In addition to their belief in the mystical possibilities of sex, the Oneida experimenters had another reason for practicing male continence. There was virtually no birth control in those days. The commune members wanted to get the most out of sex without risking unwanted pregnancies, so they sensibly reached this conclusion: no seed, no breed. Many men in those days regularly practiced *coitus interruptus* to avoid pregnancy, but the Oneida commune condemned this practice as being unfair to the women, and against the teachings of the Bible, which prohibited "spilling the seed upon the ground." They sought a way to give both partners intense sexual joy, so they developed the technique called *carezza*.

Most men and some doctors will claim that withholding semen is dangerous to a man's mental and physical health. It will cause nervous reactions, prostate trouble, urinary-tract trouble, and all manner of ailments, they say. *Carezza* proponents argue that the opposite is true—that it leads to a feeling of energetic well-being that is the reverse of the depleted, tired feeling that orgasm brings. They claim that all men will occasionally fail at *carezza* and ejaculate anyway, no matter how hard they try not to, and that the number of failures is enough to drain the seminal tubes and prevent congestion. Any other orgasms are not really necessary.

Proponents of sexual equality are increasingly favoring the concept of *carezza* today because it makes the male's sexual experience more like the female's. Men who perfect the *carezza* technique, they claim, will savor sex throughout their entire body, as women do, instead of solely in the genitals, as men supposedly do now. "Delocalizing" male sexual response enables men to appreciate sex without having an orgasm every time, just as women have always been able to do. Most men refuse to believe that women can do this; *carezza* aims to prove that it's possible not only for women but also for men.

Another point is that the man who runs away will live to fight another day. This is a round-about way of saying that if a man *does* succeed in delaying his ejaculation for an extended period of time, he can hope to emulate virtuosos like Aly Khan who gained a fantastic reputation for making love to a woman virtually all night long and giving her multiple orgasms without seeming to wear himself out. (You can always quietly collapse by yourself after you've said a fond goodnight to her.)

What do I personally think about *carezza?* The same thing as Dr. Kinsey would have thought about it: it's bad for business. Kinsey counted what he called "outlets"—and I counted money. Both of us were interested in the number of male orgasms we would rack up, the more the merrier, he for his science, me for my profession. I'm also certain that the notorious madam Mamie Stover would have suffered coronary arrest at the mere thought of a man who could go for two hours and never come. Her famous "bull ring" (4 sailors $+$ 4 partitions $\times$ 1 minute each $=$ \$20) could *never* have operated so successfully in Hawaii in those World War II days. The remarkable turnover she achieved would have ground to a stop in no time.

So *carezza* is hardly Hooker Heaven, but it is an unearthly delight. After all, I'm no longer a hooker, although I'm still happy, and so I can now take a more objective view of *carezza*. Let's continue with our lessons in the art of sustained love-making. While I address myself primarily to the man, since he's in the driver's seat in this situation, the woman is hardly uninvolved.

Klutzproof Carezza-ing

1. Don't think of orgasm as a mishap. Ejaculation doesn't end the game. It just means you have to go back to square one. Do *not* view it as a gross failure of your sexual technique. Dreading an ejaculation will merely put you in such a high state of tension that you'll be likely to have one. Simply tell yourself that you'd rather not have one. If you do, just play it again, Sam.

2. Be positive rather than negative in your determination to stay dry. Remember, you're not in a TV commercial; don't grit your teeth and say, "I will not come . . . I will not come." Instead, say "I will enjoy this wonderful act of lovemaking whether I come or not—but I'll enjoy it longer if I don't come for a long time." Don't *say* it, of course, just think it.

3. Sexuality vs. animality. From the moment you begin foreplay, keep your fondling light and feathery, mere brushstrokes. This will remove the aura of male urgency from your outward actions, and thus afford release and relaxation.

It's essential that the woman remain completely passive and relaxed. Wriggling, writhing, and other abandoned sexual movements will only defeat your man's purpose. Be voluptuous rather than hot; want *him* rather than *it*. After all, sexual response isn't confined to the area between the legs. As I mentioned, *carezza* will teach *him* that his entire body can respond to sex, just as yours does. So give him a chance. Above all, don't get desperate and beg him to let loose and give you your due share. For a change, that's exactly what he's trying to do. Luxuriate in it sensually, the way you would in a long hot bath.

Vital to remember: *forget* all those vaginal-tightening exercises you spent so many hours practicing. One or two good squeezes—and there goes his *carezza* right down your drain.

4. Change positions often. Monotony increases the chances of ejaculation because it increases steady rhythm. Nonrhythmic thrusts will help you last longer; do in bed what you shouldn't do on the dance floor—deliberately try *not* to keep time. As soon as you feel yourself slipping into a natural rhythm, stop entirely and change to another position. If you're nimble enough to change positions without disengaging from your partner, fine. If not, withdraw first and then change.

5. If you fail, make it an incomplete failure. If, after penetration, you feel an ejaculation coming on, pull out and have it *on* your lover rather than *in* her. *Coitus interruptus* is an incomplete act of love, and thus carries less finality than an ejaculation inside the vagina. Again, use psychology on yourself whenever possible. Afterward, wait one hour, urinate in order to empty the bladder entirely, and try again.

6. The third time will probably be the charm. Each ejaculation comes from one or the other testicle. Thus, if you fail in *carezza* twice, you're probably drained. Your third erection will have

the most staying power, so pin your hopes on the magic third.

Stop-Go Secrets of the Pros

Prolonged sex, which is bad for business for female hustlers, is pure gold for male ones. Street boys, gigolos, and other males for hire have used a form of *carezza* for a long time, simply because they have no choice. I've known male prostitutes who can service as many as a dozen customers a day. A man who gets into the habit of withdrawing while he's still hard will eventually develop an ability to stay half-hard even after an ejaculation.

Carezza practioners claim that it's easy to keep going for two hours, and to repeat this marathon three to five times within a twenty-four-hour period. If you have this kind of success, I can only recommend what I've been saying all along: *lubricate!* You must think this is my theme song, and it is because I get very dry in marathon sex.

If for some reason you're unable to master these techniques, or if you're too lazy to bother to learn, there's an easy way to keep it going long after it's come and gone. An effortless way of having a sexual marathon is to buy a hollow dildo that straps on. The penis is inserted in the tube, and you can last as long as you (and she) want. The penis is stimulated by being inside the cushiony, wet-feeling interior of the dildo, which will encourage another erection before too long.

Any kind of nonstop intercourse, whatever it's called, benefits a woman because it makes her feel confident of an eventual orgasm. She quickly gets used to such stellar performances and so stops worrying about whether she'll be able to make it. Once she stops worrying, she probably will make it more easily, even in much shorter lovemaking sessions.

Nonstop intercourse benefits men because it accustoms them to showing tenderness and consideration—always a good lesson for anyone to learn. And anything new on the lovemaking front will tune each of you into a new side of your lover.

However, many women find that too constant a virtuoso performance can be too much of a good thing. Paradoxically, too much painstaking sexual attention can dehumanize a woman as much as the wham-bam-thank-you-ma'am kind. She begins to feel like an instrument being tuned by a compulsive fiddler. At times like this, another approach is called for—creative *in*continence, better known as the quickie. And *that* brings us to the next chapter.

13. The Quickie; or Minute Man Meets Minute Maid

When you're a Happy Hooker, you're in a fast-delivery business, just the way McDonald's is in the fast-food business. There's no time for those long, leisurely, elegant meals with four courses of foreplay before the *pièce de résistance*.

Nevertheless, I know lots of people who remember fondly, as a delicious food experience in their lives, a Big Mac gobbled down in thirty seconds flat, halfway home on the long drive down Route 66. Likewise, if you're rushed for time, or if you're so famished you can't wait, the quickie can be the most powerful form of sex of all the fifty-seven (or is it sixty-nine?) varieties.

Personally speaking, I prefer leisurely lovemaking, but I also favor a change of pace once in a while. Sometimes you have to do things differently if you want the spice for which variety is famous. Now that I've instructed you in the art of nonstop lovemaking, I'm going to give equal time to the case for the quickie.

I've had many quickies in my time, of course. When I was a hooker, they were par for the course because time is money in that business (as in most other businesses). Busy executives were always running into my house, for a quick business transaction—and running out again. I expected it, accepted it, and felt no resentment at being the "ma'am" in wham-bam-thank-you-ma'am.

The quickie, needless to say, is hardly an American invention. For example, Hedrick Smith, in his book *The Russians*, points out that American bachelors in Moscow are valued as lovers because, as he says, "In Russia lovemaking has a slam-bam-thank-you-ma'am quality. This may be because so many people live in apartments and dormitories where privacy is difficult. Foreplay is seen as a Western invention, and it is appreciated very much."

Incidentally, in case you're planning a trip to the USSR, he also says, "Publicly the Russians seem very puritanical and prudish, but behind that, the sex life abounds. Promiscuity is all over the place."

Accepting the quickie in personal relationships is something else. Now that women have discovered the full extent of their sexuality, they tend to demand thorough sexual servicing and refuse to be "used" by impatient, importunate men.

Women's new demands for pleasure have made many men secretly long for the good old days when they were free to "have their way" with women without worrying about orgasms, lubrication, erect nipples or performing a ring-and-valve job on the clitoris. Things have come to such a pass that one man I know recently said to me, "If I hear one more goddam word about the clitoris, I'm going to enter a Trappist monastery."

Frankly, I think that men and women in every age have been indoctrinated into thinking what they're "supposed" to think. These days, a woman

believes that a quickie is sacrilege, and a man believes that if God doesn't get him for it, his
woman will. Our Puritan ancestors believed that
sex was evil because that's what they were supposed to believe, just as many of us believed
parents when they told us we'd go blind and get
acne if we masturbated. (The only consolation was
that at least we wouldn't have to look at ourselves.) Fortunately, many of us listened to our
bodies instead of our parents. So why stop now?
An old wives' tale is an old wives' tale, whether
it's told by a Mrs. or a Ms.

I don't recommend it as a steady diet, but there
are times for men *and* women when a quickie is
exactly what the body and psyche need. Most
women are too solicitious of their new freedom to
admit it, but there are times when the female of
the species needs and wants sex without ceremony.

What are some of these times?

When She Feels More Bitchy than Itchy

The quickie can be an ego-booster or reinforcer
for a woman as much as for a man. It's a matter of
saying "Look what I can do to a man!" While a
man may use a quickie to prove his potency and
masculinity, a woman will often use his beat-the-
clock lust to prove to herself, as well as to him,
how irresistible *she* is.

Sometimes a woman wants to make love; other
times, she wants sex. In the first instance, she cares
about her own pleasure and wants to have an orgasm; in the second, she's motivated by narcissism

and wants to flex her ego and celebrate the self. In plain talk, she wants to show off.

In more puritanical times, this mood was hinted at in the many stories about the woman who bought a new hat when she felt blue. The impulse purchase was a respectable substitute for the quick, crazy, shocking sex that she *really* wanted but could not admit she wanted, even to herself. Nowadays women know themselves better and are permitted to be more blunt about their needs. The woman who uses a shopping trip as an ego boost will now buy a sexy nightgown instead of a hat. Once she owns it and takes it home and models it, her renewed narcissism takes the form of seductiveness. She's not hot in the strict sense of the word, but a quick tumble in bed will prove her seductiveness and bolster her morale.

A quickie is also in order when her ego is at a high. *Any* victory in a woman's life, whether it's a successful diet, new clothes, or just an unusually good day in general, will make her feel desirable. What she actually feels between her legs has nothing to do with it. At such times, she loves nothing better than to be "taken," as they used to say.

So the next time your girlfriend gets a raise, a promotion, or loses ten pounds—grab her for a quickie!

When She Feels More Greedy than Needy

Women are more prudent than men; we hate to waste anything. A warm spring night, a deserted field or beach, a full moon, and a brief but violent thunderstorm are all sexy times. Any situation that reminds her of sex, or even more, anything that triggers a specific sexual memory, is a psychological turn-on. Especially potent is a situation or a setting that reminds her of a *missed chance* in the past: she didn't make love five years ago on that other moonlit beach, she's regretted it ever since, so she's going to by-God take advantage of *this* one *now*.

This is the motivation of the cool and contained woman who suddenly turns to a man and moans "Do it to me!" Her puzzled lover never knows what has gotten into her. Usually, he makes the mistake of asking a question or making a comment, thus ruining the spontaneity that she wants.

Xaviera's principle in this situation: "Don't ask—just act fast!"

When She's Bored and Wants to Be Floored

As I've said before, the famous—or infamous— rape fantasy is not really a desire to be raped *per se*. No woman actually wants to be raped, but every woman does want to be "swept off her feet," to use a Victorian expression. How else do you account for the fact that every other woman you see on a bus or subway these days is reading an erotic gothic novel?

As every man knows, women are contrary critters. Hard as it is to believe, a woman may at times get angry at a man for being too much the considerate gentleman in bed.

Too much thoroughness and organization in a man will upset a woman on a subconscious level. There comes a point when an overly careful man is no longer much of one in her eyes. Too much precision and patience in foreplay are vaguely reminiscent of the fussy bachelor who straightens pictures, stacks newspapers in perfect alignment, and saves string. A man who is too solicitous *all* the time is brushing close to being "an old maid in breeches." Given a choice between a buccaneer and a bookkeeper, most women will chose the lusty pirate.

The big problem for a man is to know just *when* a woman is feeling bored and desirous of surprise. Believe it or not, it's easy to figure out. Every man has seen the famous signs and been needlessly puzzled by them, giving rise to that famous male question: "What's the matter?" To which a woman invariably replies, "Nothing." After this exchange, her disposition may go into high-gear barracuda and erupt into irrational attacks on his personal habits. "Stop twisting your mouth like that when you chew!" . . . "If you rattle your ice one more time, I'll scream!"

Most men blame this on the time of the month, but that's too pat. A woman in this kind of mood is weary of civilized men; she's had too much male *consideration*. The cure is obvious. She needs a fast-delivery specialist, and only a supersonic transport will do.

When She's in the Mood for a Mood-Swap

Women have a way of springing good-natured-
ness on a man, too. A woman will gladly participate in a quickie when she senses that her man is
desperately horny; she doesn't have the heart to
make him delay his satisfaction to warm her up.
Actually, she isn't being all *that* kind; it's just that
women have a great deal of imagination. A man's
physical urgency, if it's powerful enough, can be
translated into a woman's psychological urgency.
In other words, it's catching. She "becomes" the
man in a kind of mood-swap of personality exchange.

When He's Hot and She's Not

The average woman feels anything but sexy a
few days before her period starts, when she feels
bloated and swollen. This is not a sexy feeling,
but it's a very female feeling because premenstrual bodily changes simulate pregnancy. She's
heavy, and actually feels much bigger physically
than at other times, very much like an overweight
earth goddess.

The woman who feels lethargic rather than dis-
tasteful to herself at this time is a good candidate
for a quickie. It will make her feel like a rather
billowy, pillowy sex symbol. (It's also good for her
morale.)

Quickie Ground Rules

1. Keep your shirt on. The whole idea behind the quickie is destroyed if you both get completely undressed. You can have nude sex anytime; in a quickie, the name of the game is *urgency*.

If your woman is wearing a long robe, open it but don't let her take it off. If she's in slacks, pull them and her panty hose down but don't remove them. There's something sexy about clothes bunching around the ankles. The most important thing to remember is: don't take off your pants! Nudity has become so commonplace that women are starting to get a thrill out of seeing a naked penis sticking out on a fully dressed man.

2. The bedroom is off limits. Remember that you're doing things differently. The bed will still be there when you revert to your customary lovemaking. The quickie should be free of all premeditation. Standing up in the kitchen while dinner is cooking away on the stove—or better still, when guests are waiting in the living room—adds an element of danger. (See if you can beat the pressure cooker.) I once had a terrific quick dip on a beach cabana when my guy and I went in to change bathing suits. I bent down to slip my wet suit off, and whango, there was a warm and eager penis in my still cold and damp behind.

3. The missionary position is out. This tried-and-true standby is simply too tried and true for anything as radical as a quickie. For the quickie, I recommend the rear-entry position. There are

several reasons why this is psychologically smart. First, it's better for a man not to see a familiar face, thereby futhering the illusion of a "zipless fuck" with a complete stranger. Second, the woman can give him sex without giving him the whole person, thus preserving the sheer carnality of the act. Finally, if she should feel guilty for some reason, she can tell herself, in effect, "It wasn't my doing; he came up behind me." (Like a thief in the night.)

The beat-the-clock repertoire can be performed around the clock. It can include the morning glory, the coffee break or matinee, the predinner appetizer, and the commercial break. The desk job can easily be performed on the kitchen or dining-room table. Sex in public (or in an unaccustomed place) also lends itself to the quickie, because the excitement of the situation means that extensive foreplay isn't necessary—or even wanted.

As long as the quickie doesn't become a habit, there's nothing "second-class" about it. It's just as "good" as the more expert, drawn-out kind of sex you enjoy most of the time. It offers a change of pace indulged in by some very renowned people. The most famous quickie is undoubtedly that enjoyed by President Warren Harding and his mistress, Nan Britten, in the White House linen closet. That's one way of saving the sheets!

There's definitely something about the possibility of danger and discovery that adds a certain fillip to rapid-fire performances. A quickie that involves these elements fulfills something elemental in the human soul that we all harbor. It certainly keeps the adrenaline flowing, so it could be said that quickies are good for you!

Another benefit of the quickie is that it builds self-assurance in a man with premature-ejaculation or impotency problems. If he knows that he needn't worry about the woman's pleasure—either because she gets a bang out of a quickie or because she's willing to forego the bang on occasion in the interest of bigger and better bangs in the future—he'll gain confidence and eventually solve his problems.

Finally, a quickie has an element of humor in it that makes sex fun. Sometimes a long, drawn-out virtuoso bed performance can get a little grim, as any form of painstaking perfection will, so enjoy a quickie now and then—like the entertaining short subjects at the movies that often outshine the two-hour feature film.

Above all, don't hesitate or dillydally when you're going for a quickie. When you uncork a bottle of champagne, time is of the essence. Otherwise you'll lose all that effervescence!

14. Love Around the Clock; or It's Always Sex O'Clock

It seems that every nationality has a favorite time for lovemaking. The French prefer *cinq à sept*, five to seven P.M., for their adulterous *liaisons dangereuses*, when businessmen detour from their homeward trek to stop by at their mistresses' apartments. *L'heure bleue*, they call it, for the blue twilight time. (This particular custom of social and other forms of intercourse has led to late dinners and a rush hour that's two hours later than the international average.)

Italians, at least to judge from the preference of my old Mafia customers in New York, like to punch in—and out—as early in the morning as possible. I had Dom "the Gat" and Al "the Banana" at seven or eight A.M. Either they had been out all night and stopped by my house on their way home, en route to early Mass, or else they were planning a shoot-out later in the day and wanted to shoot what might be their last wad first.

I don't really know about the Irish, but if you want to go by national stereotypes, it would depend on the hours of their favorite pub. That comes first; they work everything else around their drinking.

Despite the diversity of American life, this is

basically an Anglo-Saxon country, so most Americans tend to follow English sex patterns. England may swing, as the song says, but her underpinnings are essentially puritanical, and Americans have copied them unconsciously. Most Americans still feel that nighttime is sex time and that the glare of daylight makes sex glaringly wicked.

I'm convinced that many Americans make love at bedtime before going to sleep so that they can lapse into unconsciousness afterward and avoid, for a few hours at least, the sense of guilt they feel about having sex at all. If they save sex for last, they won't have to face each other until breakfast, when the activities of busy family life will distract them as they go about the favorite American custom of hurrying off to work.

Actually, much sexual failure can be attributed to bedtime sex. What worse time, really, could a couple pick? You're tired, probably full of indigestible late-night snacks, and your erotic mood has been dampened by Johnny Carson's monolog.

If we can set aside time for homework, self-improvement, and hobbies, why can't we also set aside time for sex?

Peak Time

When I had my house in New York, I was at first amazed to find that my peak business hour was between three and four in the afternoon. I wondered why this should be so; finally I asked a regular customer, who always arrived on the dot at three, why he was compulsive about that particular hour.

"Think a minute," he said with a grin. "What does three o'clock mean?"

The light dawned. "Why, that's when school lets out," I said in a bemused voice.

He nodded. "Relaxation—and freedom—begin at three in the afternoon."

Think about it; it makes sense. Don't people in offices unconsciously start getting restless around three? Isn't that when the afternoon coffee break is scheduled? The reason is everyone's internal time clock. We've all gone to school, and the child within us feels good at three o'clock. What better time, then, for sex?

Admittedly, it's a little hard to manage on a nine-to-five working schedule, but once in a while you can knock off early and make up the time later, can't you? Far more conventional authors than I recommend an interruption of the workday for sex; the author of *The Total Woman*, wife and mother Marabel Morgan, recommends calling your husband at the office and saying: "I crave your body." The idea is to get him to drop what he's doing and come home—to come *at* home.

If you do this too often, of course, you'll soon be able to spend all day, every day at home, running through your unemployment insurance. But for an occasional change of pace, try a mid-afternoon variation.

The Naked Lunch

With a bow to Helen Gurley Brown, editor-in-chief of *Cosmopolitan*, who first told a shocked America about lunchtime sex in *Sex and the Single Girl* and *Sex and the Office,* this can be fairly easy to manage, since everyone gets at least an hour for lunch, and most people take more time than they get.

The advantages of the matinee are obvious. First, it's slimming, because you really don't have time to eat a complete meal, and since sex is emotionally filling, you may want to skip lunch entirely. Second, it's a perfect compromise time for both A.M. and P.M. personality types. Depending on your metabolic makeup, you come alive either early in the day or much later. Lunchtime finds almost everyone alert and vigorous; the night person has gotten over his morning grumps, and the day person has come down somewhat from his euphoric morning glories. (Lunchtime may be the only time that these two types can *stand* each other.) Another advantage is that lunchtime sex can do more to cure puritanical hang-ups than anything I know of. You can't hide in the dark at high noon; whatever way your apartment windows face, there's plenty of daylight to come streaming in, even if you close the draperies. A break for those who get a thrill out of the forbidden is that most apartment buildings are virtually emptied of people during the day, so a lunchtime sex date thus takes on qualities of stealth that

make you feel wicked, like two lovers sneaking
into a deserted castle.

While too much haste can ruin sex, too much
leisure can dampen the fun, too. A matinee idyll
requires just the right amount of hurrying to elec-
trify both partners and impart a sense of urgency
that makes for more fun.

Don't Screw Up the High-Noon Shoot-Out

Never attend a matinee unless you live reason-
ably close to your office or can arrange for a con-
venient rendezvous. Racing down U.S. 90 in a
state of heat can cause you to wrap yourselves
around a telephone pole instead of each other.
Even a minor accident can cause serious reverber-
ations if both of you are married to other people;
police keep records and ask a lot of questions,
remember. If you *must* drive all the way out to
Shady Knolls, use two cars. Otherwise, go to a ho-
tel near where you work, or borrow an apartment
from an understanding friend. A bachelor friend
of the man's is the best bet; girlfriends tend to get
jealous of all the fun that someone else is having
in *their* beds. They're also likely to feel more fastidious about what happens there, no matter how
carefully the lovers tidy up.

If your apartment or home is the spot, remember to make your bed in the morning before leav-
ing the house. There's no greater turn-off than
being greeted by a rumpled bed in the middle of
the day.

Above all, *don't* change your clothes before you

return to the office after a lunchtime sex bout. Everybody will know you've been home, and they'll immediately jump to the correct conclusion. If you can't have fun without everybody's knowing about it, you've got problems. That's a form of "indecent exposure" anyone can avoid—unless he wants to show off.

The Morning Glory

This is just a guess, but in my case, any guess on the subject of sex is bound to be an educated one. It seems to me that more men are "morning types" than women. Perhaps it's because women are supposedly geared to the cycles of the moon and thus respond more to everything after dark. It's also possible that men have been culturally conditioned to be morning people because they've been the breadwinners for so many centuries; if the early bird gets the worm, then the early worm gets the bird, especially when it wakes up with an erection, as it usually does.

Early-morning sex delights both sexes for different reasons. In many ways it's an ideal time for sex. The morning hard-on is the easiest erection of all; many men who find it difficult instead of hard at other times wake up with one every day. It starts during sleep, when all anxiety is at a minimum, and so the man wakes up with a *fait accompli:* for once, he doesn't have to worry about whether he *will* get an erection—he already has one. Successfully negotiating morning sex can do wonders for the man with potency problems.

Women are especially receptive to morning sex in a way that's calculated to soothe any male. Women tend to be cuddly in the morning; they may be in the mood for sex, but it's not a demanding mood. Even the most aggressive women experience these passive morning moments.

Morning sex is also aided by the sleeping positions favored by the two sexes. Men generally sleep on their backs (which is why they snore). Most women do little sleeping on their backs, perhaps because it's a defenseless position for them. Nor do women feel comfortable sleeping on their stomachs, because it hurts their breasts. A woman might avoid this by putting an arm (hers) under herself, but the arm would get numb and thus wake her up. The logical outcome of these physiological facts is that women are great side-sleepers, which means that a man has a fifty-fifty chance of finding his woman already in position for an arousing arousal.

Suddenly It Springs

Taking a woman without warning appeals to men because it makes them feel aggressive. The average woman enjoys this kind of male dominance because of the surprise element and because she occasionally enjoys a touch of the primitive he-man in her lover. But if he happens to catch her when she isn't so inclined, at least it doesn't detract from her pride. She can tell herself that it happened while she was asleep and so she wasn't responsible.

The most important rule for a morning glory is directed at the woman: *Let him do it!* Denying a man who has achieved an effortless erection is dangerous business; if he's rejected often enough at such moments, his future erections may require a great deal of effort. Remember, this is his most masculine moment; he woke up, and there it was, hard as a rock. Rejecting his lovemaking forces him to waste something very valuable to him. All she need do, if she doesn't feel like doing anything else, is raise her top leg enough so that he can get in from behind.

If she wants to enjoy a little counterrevolutionary coyness—and every woman does from time to time—she can pretend she was asleep the whole time, and have some fun at breakfast playing the innocent. A man who goes off to work wondering *Did she really not remember it?* is an intrigued man. Since it's getting more and more difficult to intrigue men these days, I heartily recommend this ploy.

The Appetizer

Now that we have timed ovens, the two of you can get things cooking without worrying about burning the dinner. Predinner sex is such a logical thing to me; after all, even the stuffiest people recognize this period of the day as a time for relaxation. These days, a little wickedness in the form of a cocktail or three is par for the course even in superrespectable small towns. It's only a hop, skip, and jump-in-the-feathers to include sex in this all-American ritual.

The problem with predinner sex is that someone else may be around—like the kids. The best way to get rid of your small audience is to get them all a paper route. If this doesn't work, send them upstairs to do their homework, and hope for the best.

Even if you haven't been blessed with any little bundles from what's-that-place, predinner sex still presents problems. Quite often you're either going out somewhere right after dinner, or friends are scheduled to stop by. A real hell-for-leather sex session results in mussed hair and requires a shower and change of clothes. Since you don't want to feel harassed, you might not want to go the limit at this time.

Which is why predinnertime is ideal for fellatio. Most men are strung out when they get home from work anyhow; they need sex to unwind, but they're also tired. This is when a woman who knows how to schedule things can make her man eternally grateful—so grateful that he'll return the favor in spades at some other time, which makes up for any frustration she might feel if she doesn't get hers before the meatloaf is done.

A great place to go down on a man before dinner is in the kitchen, with the help of a tall step stool. No one who happens to enter the kitchen will actually see what's going on. They'll just think you're leaning over to get something out of a cabinet. Give your man a drink and let him relax and enjoy!

And Now a Pause for ...

You've got to do *something* during TV commercials, don't you? If you don't want to risk missing part of the show (do you really care?) , you can use these station breaks for gentle, leisurely fondling.

The real test comes at football time. Don't try to distract him during the game. Even Raquel Welch would come in a distant second. Wait until the first half ends and then go to work. You have twenty minutes to waylay him. And if you can make him forget to turn on the set for the start of the second half, give yourself six points plus a big pat on the back.

On a nonfootball program, remember to pick your commercials carefully. For example, most men find it impossible to get an erection during the chain-saw ads where they go "Zzzzzz!" and the log is sliced down the middle.

If you can manage to keep a man sexed up during TV viewing, he'll be completely primed when you turn the set off. Remember, he's a lot like an old-fashioned TV set himself. He has to be warmed up first. They haven't started making solid-state men yet.

15. Sex Is Where You Find It; or If You Can't Change the Faces, Change the Places

Edwardian England's favorite actress, Mrs. Patrick Campbell, once said, "It doesn't matter what people do in the bedroom so long as they don't do it in the streets and frighten the horses."

Times have changed with a bang. People are now doing it while riding horses. They're also doing it in sleeping bags, Greyhound buses, laundromats, shopping centers, airplane toilets, or, like Erica Jong's heroine, in supposedly sacred locations. (A little blasphemy goes a long way.) Isadora Wing in *Fear of Flying* chose the Jewish chapel on the *Queen Mary*—because it was always empty.

Sex in public or semipublic places is the latest thing. We don't have to look far for the reason: danger always adds a fillip to sex—and in these liberated days, there aren't any dangers left, to speak of. Gone are the dangers of pregnancy, disgrace, stoning of adulterers, and the wearing of the scarlet letter. Severe as these punishments were, they answered a certain perverse need for adventurous challenge that lurks in the human soul. Permissiveness, for all its attractions, falls short in this regard: there are no challenges left, so we must invent them.

Actually, having sex in odd places is not nearly so newfangled as we would like to believe. In fact, the original Puritans did it. In the Massachusetts Bay Colony in the seventeenth century, a couple enjoyed some unholy sex in an empty church. Their union proved fruitful, so they named the baby boy Bench, in honor of the place on which he was conceived.

In the prejet age, passengers on leisurely ocean cruises used the lifeboats. In Tennessee Williams' novel *The Roman Spring of Mrs. Stone*, the actress heroine used her dressing room between the acts—and between the comings and goings of her wardrobe lady. In the Swedish movie *I Am Curious, Yellow*, a young man had his girl on the fence in front of the royal palace, with a sentry standing at attention nearby. Which all goes to prove that there's more to it than just "my place or yours?"

There are several advantages to making it in strange places. First, the tension and fear of discovery that build up make the sex better than the garden-variety boudoir kind. We have heard so much about restful, ideal settings that we forget they can also take the edge off pleasure—or even ability. Contrary to popular opinion, fear need not cause impotency. Quite the contrary; it's a well-known fact that men on battlefields can get automatic erections from sheer fright. As for women, the muscular tightening that we all experience during danger can trigger convulsive vaginal palpitations.

Oddly enough, once you've braved the danger of public sex, sex in privacy becomes more exciting. Your self-image improves, you feel daring and clever—in other words, success breeds success. You also come to appreciate comfort and privacy more after you've experienced the sweet rigors of sex in a telephone booth or a parking ramp.

Being daring is one thing; being arrested is something else. Yet there is little possibility of any real trouble. In the first place, the very people who would be offended by your activities are bluenoses who couldn't bring themselves to *mention* such things to policemen or other authorities. Also, few people are willing to risk the "sour-grapes" tag that would very likely be pinned on them if they reported you. The average person will either ignore you or watch you. The worst that could happen is being stuck with a kibitzer who decides he'd like to join the fun.

The most colorful instance of out-of-the-way sex I've heard of is the story of the Pennsylvania Turnpike. A female toll collector was caught making it with a truck driver in the toll booth.

What better place to get your ticket punched? There's no rest for the resourceful, but here are a few suggestions to give you the general idea of it all.

Bare-Assed Bareback

Horses are easily frightened, but they're also dumb. As long as they don't actually see what's going on, they stay cool and collected.

A girl I know regularly has intercourse while riding bareback. (And it isn't only the horse whose back is bare.) She sits in front, naked from the waist down, and leans far forward over the horse's neck. Her lover mounts behind her with his arms about her waist—and then uses her rear entry. The movements of a slow trot are enough to bring them both off; they don't have to do a thing except *be* there.

Warning: you both must be *extremely* good horsemen. In other words, you'd better be damn sure you know as much about equitation as you do about fornication.

Post No Bills

A construction site surrounded by a boarded-up fence containing holes for sidewalk superintendents to peep through. Until recently, the sexiest sight available was that of Mugsy O'Leary and his pneumatic drill, but times have changed. If you like to be watched but don't care to see the watchers, this is an ideal place. *They* can see everything, but *you* can see nothing but unblinking eyes.

Snorkel Sex

The advantages of deep-sea sex are obvious. (The disadvantage is that it doesn't work most of the time, the penis not having been designed to write under water.) In a natural setting, you have beautiful tropical colors and craggy coral castles all around you. You're weightless under water, so you can try out all the crazy positions you can't manage on terra firma. You also might stimulate each other's genitals with a whoosh of tickly bubbles from your air tubes.

Other possible disadvantages? Well, there's *Jaws*. Remember, too, that water, if it's too cold, has a tendency to shrivel the penis. Even if the man manages to get an erection, the water will make it twice as difficult to enter the vagina. Water tightens the vagina, and also washes out the natural juices.

If you confine your snorkel sex to the warm waters of the Caribbean, you'll be better off. Otherwise, keep in mind the old skinny-dipper's joke: "Oh, look, the water is *that* cold!" they say, as they measure one inch with thumb and forefinger.

Transcendental Meditation

Most churches these days, especially in big cities, are kept locked against robbers and vandals. But airports and many hotels offer what they call a "mediatation room," or, if they call a spade a spade, a chapel. I once missed a plane in Seattle and spent three hours in the meditation room, all by my lonesome. Not a soul came near it. Apparently, all the men looking for girls were in the bar. Little did they know that the Happy Hooker was in the chapel, just waiting to answer a few fevered prayers. Better luck next time, fellows. As

for me, I wound up indulging my own version
of TM—transcendental masturbation.

Do Fence Him In

I'm fascinated with hammocks, particularly the
net kind with holes. A man lying in the hammock
on his stomach with his penis stuck through a hole
is one of my favorite fantasies. I'm lying on my
back on the ground, with my deep throat at the
ready.

A girl who worked for me once happened to
find herself near a prison farm one day when she
ran out of gas on a dusty Southern road. The few
prisoners and the sleepy guard were enclosed in a
wire fence with octagonal holes in it. While the
guard slept peacefully through the heat of the
day, she generated some heat of her own with the
prisoners. Each of them stuck his penis through a
hole and she gave equal time to each. She ended
the day with octagonal designs burned into her
rump from having backed up against the fence
doggy-style. She also collected about fifteen bucks
in small change for her acts of mercy.

The "imprisoned-man" fantasy is a favorite of
many women. If you get a thrill from calling the
shots with a helpless man, you can imitate my
friend's experiences. All you need is a fence with a
narrow aperture of some kind, plus a guy to
"mesh" around with. A man with a fairly thick
penis derives a bonus pleasure from this game;
once he gets an erection, he can't excape from the
hole until he comes. While he's trapped in it, it

feels like a penis ring and increases his throbbing sensations.

If Rear-View Mirrors Could Talk

A great many women have a strong urge to go down on a man in the back seat of a cab. I think the reason for this has to do with the cabdriver; he's an authority figure in a way, and his back is turned. Perhaps he represents the woman's father, whom she has always longed to shock with a sexual escapade, but had to content herself with "going behind his back."

Taxis have long been trysting places, because drivers don't care what you do as long as you pay the fare. If you do naughty things, he knows that he'll get a bigger tip for ignoring the situation, so a taxi is a good place to begin your adventure into semipublic sex.

If you want to keep things on a one-to-one basis, it's best not to pick a young, long-haired driver— he might look in his rear-vision mirror and want to join the fun. Stick with the older Archie Bunker types. They won't say a word to the naughty passengers; they'll just rant and rave to their families when they get off duty.

Library of Congress

Libraries have more to offer than books. There are dark nooks and crannies, basement stacks, back-issue rooms, and stepladders.

Cunnilingus on a ladder might be called sexual climbing—there's more than one way to get up there. It also looks very scholarly, because people who use ladders in libraries are usually after some rare volume that's so unpopular or unreadable that it's kept on the very top shelf.

If the librarian is hanging around and you want to get rid of her, ask her to find you a copy of any of the following titles: *The Art of English Cooking*, *Italian War Heroes*, *The Presbyterian Church of Spain*, or *The Complete History of Jewish Alcoholism*.

The Art of Friction

Now that touch dancing is coming back, you can enjoy a crazy-making nostalgia craze. In days gone by, this practice used to result in lots of cleaning bills for the man. Now that both sexes wear fly-front pants, you can get even closer to "the real thing" with very little risk of being discovered.

Remember to leave off underwear. Open both flies and insert your penis into your girl's pants. You won't be able to enter her vagina, but on a crowded dance floor you can do a lot just the same. Slide it through her vaginal lips or thrust it between her legs and then weave slowly to the music while she squeezes you rhythmically. If a nearby couple bangs into you, *watch out!*

As I wrote in one of my other books, an unknown and unseen man who danced behind me as I was dancing with my partner once tried this approach. With all due modesty, I must say that this is probably the ultimate in public displays. It certainly proves Edgar Allan Poe's theory: "The safest hiding place is the most obvious one."

16. Gimmicks, Gadgets, Stabbers, and Grabbers; or More Power to You

Not so long ago, the only sex toys that most people knew about were dildos and French ticklers. And half the people who "knew" about them only *thought* they knew. In fact, these two artifacts were so well cloaked in mystery and censorship that hardly anyone had ever seen them, let alone used them, and several misguided legends grew up around them. Dildos were said to be used exclusively by old men, or by men who had "dissipated" themselves so thoroughly that they were victims of "lost manhood." In spite of the dictates of the obvious, no one seemed to realize that lesbians also used them.

The lore surrounding French ticklers was even more incredible. Like Spanish fly, they were said to be used by villainous male seducers on unsuspecting virgins. The prickly bumps were supposed to "change" said virgins from healthy, clean-minded girls to insatiable nymphomaniacs. As the saying put it: "Once a woman knows what a French tickler feels like, she'll never be satisfied any other way."

Nowadays we know that using sex aids is nothing to be ashamed of, and there's nothing "addictive" about it unless you want to be addicted.

They don't imply impotence or lead to depravity, any more than a cocktail before dinner makes a person an alcoholic. It's just an apéritif, something to be enjoyed from time to time to increase one's pleasure in the main course.

Sex toys have been around longer than most people realize. Archaeologists have found artificial penises in Egyptian tombs, and cave drawings suggest that similar equipment was in use as much as forty thousand years ago! Nor are sex gimmicks and gadgets evidence of a breakdown in civilization; during the golden age of France, at the height of that country's culture, Louis XV had a "jiggling chair," called the *trémoussoir*, that provided a below-the-waist massage much like today's vibrators. The philosopher Voltaire used to borrow it from time to time, and sat happily turning the crank while he relaxed his genius. And the Japanese have had a refined and sophisticated collection of sexual titillators for hundreds of years.

The Japanese are, of course, preeminent in the invention and manufacture of modern sex aids as well. Today, the sex-toy business has ejaculated into a forty-million-dollar annual business in this country alone.

One day recently a well-dressed woman walked into a Manhattan boutique and bought a vibrator. She didn't buy it as a gift, a party joke, or "for my bad back." She bought it, she freely admitted, "to use when my husband and I make love."

Five years ago, such a woman wouldn't even have discussed the topic of sex aids. But today, multitudes of people in her social class are snatching up sex products once consigned to the back pages of seamy magazines. They don't have to disguise themselves when they go shopping, either. They can now shop in posh stores with piped-in music instead of resorting to under-the-counter establishments in under-the-rock neighborhoods.

Of all the new devices, the vibrator is unquestionably the most popular and widely purchased. It accounts for more than half of the volume of "marital aids" sold.

Good Vibrations

Recently a warm-blooded, sex-loving girl wrote to me about a serious problem. She seemed to be an intelligent girl, except that she was a little shaky on Greek myths. She signed herself "Pig Malion" and explained that she had fallen in love with her vibrator.

Ever since the Greek sculptor Pygmalion fell in love with his female creation, men have lived in danger of falling in love with an impossible ideal. Now women have the same problem with their vibrators—the little buzzers are so good that some women seem to find them "better" than a living lover.

Psychologist Wardell Pomeroy, coauthor of the Kinsey report, says, "Many women simply can't seem to have an orgasm any way except with a vibrator." While this can be a problem, Dr. Pomeroy, like other sex therapists, is still basically optimistic. He adds, "More important, perhaps, women may eventually be able to learn from the vibrator how to have an orgasm without it."

Vibrators come in all shapes and sizes. They are penis-shaped, pistol-shaped and even egg-beater-shaped. Electrically powered models generally pulsate harder than their battery-operated brethren. If the batteries are weak, the unit may not budge at all when applied to the skin. If the gadget culminates in a weighted tip, as the standard vibrator does, it is likely to impart more sensation than a device attached to a large, flat disk. (The latter is really for aches and pains.)

Vibrators range in size from a four-and-a-half-inch "mini" to a ten-or-more-inch-long "executive model." You can spend as little as seven dollars or as much as forty, depending on the attachments.

Since the standard vibrator is penis-shaped, many women attempt to achieve vaginal orgasm by inserting the vibrator and touching the cervix with the tip. I've found—and nearly every woman I know agrees—that the effect of this is nil. The cervix is a tough, gristly musclelike organ and needs more stimulation than the bee buzz of a vibrator. Moving the vibrator in and out of the vagina doesn't work, either. The smooth-surface model lacks anything like the veins and coronal ridge of a real penis, and the fluted model is *too* ridged for comfort. Besides, it's tiring (the instrument is fairly heavy) and it puts you in a doubled-up position if you want to do a thorough job of it. Your breasts get squashed somewhere around your midriff as you bend forward, and your nipples get lost in the shuffle.

The boon of the vibrator is the whisper-soft touch it can give to the clitoris. Not even the gentlest finger can do for your clitoris what a properly applied vibrator can do. By properly applied, I mean barely touching it at all. My favorite way of using my vibrator is to lie on my back on the bed with my feet flat up against the wall. In this position, the vagina gapes open and is free to stretch at will as excitement increases. At the moment of orgasm, the entire vaginal channel flutters like a bird's wings, and you can savor the intense pulsations far better than you can during actual intercourse. (No unfavorable reflection intended on you guys; I'm just reporting my personal experience.)

Look, Three Hands!

For a really stimulating party à une, try three vibrators—count 'em, three. Spread your legs and flatten your feet against the wall. Prop one vibrator between your thighs, resting its base on a small pillow if necessary, so that it leans up against the vulva with the tip resting against your clitoris. Use the other two vibrators on your breasts. When you climax—and *believe me*, you will—you can lift your body a little so that the tip of vibrator *numero uno* slides down your vagina. At this point, you'll be wet enough to draw the tip into your body with a sucking motion that will double your pleasure.

A Powerful Attachment

Americans love to package things. *Anything!* Something in the American soul loves a neat cellophane-wrapped box (that's impossible to open without a butcher knife) containing extra little parts that screw, snap, or pop on and off. I love to watch Americans inspect a new kitful of something. They look like children on Christmas morning. They pick up each attachment and exclaim, "Oh! Here's a little this . . . and, oh, look, there's one of *those*!" Everything is a thingamabob or a whatchamacallit, and the new owner will happily put it together and take it apart for at least an hour, ignoring the pile of Styrofoam, guarantees, and warranties at his feet.

So it was inevitable that we should have a vibrator kit. And what's in it?

"Well, look at this gizmo!" A "rectifier," which is a long, curved plastic attachment that snaps into the base of the vibrator. The "rectifier" is inserted into the rectum for simultaneous anal-clitoral stimulation.

"Hey, it's got a whatsitsname!" A "slurpee," which is a vibrator sleeve with the shape and texture of a human tongue. (Yes, you heard me correctly.)

"Say, here's a whoosits!" A "nip and tuck," which consists of two small suction cups attached to wires extending from the base of the vibrator, to be attached to nipples.

"This only comes with the deluxe model!" A "Tootsie Roll," which is a three-inch flesh-colored cylinder especially molded to adjust to your individual internal dimensions, which can be worn all day long in your whatever, and which operates on an independent power supply of its own for daylong buzzing.

If anything goes wrong with anything in your

kit, you can return the whole business to the factory, which, like all factories, is located in Someplace, New Jersey 07022.

Face Value

You can't judge people or vibrators by their faces. But a face can still be a turn-on, especially if there's a good vibrator behind it. Yes, you can even buy friendly, helpful rubber masks (there's one that's a dead ringer for the "Smile" button) that look like what you wore for Halloween 'way back when, except you can turn them on for a turn-on that beats trick-or-treat by a long sight. For women there's the "Muffie," which has a long vibrating tongue, For men, there's the "Gulp," which has a long hollow tube behind the throat.

Ring Around the Penis

As you've probably guessed by now, there's a vibrator to stimulate anyone's fantasies. There are also a lot of other gadgets that you may have dreamed of in your wildest dreams, but never dreamed they really existed. Luckily, there are some practical dirty-minded inventors who have put their fantasies to down-to-earth use. (And you thought that little old man on line at the patent office looked so sweet!) Here are some other gadgets to get your gizmo going, beginning with the penis ring.

This item certainly beats a ring around the tub.

Contrary to widespread opinion, a penis ring does not *create* an erection, it simply prolongs it. You have to get it up on your own steam, then apply the ring to keep it at the ready.

There are many different kinds of penis rings, from the leather thongs used by the Japanese to the newer "Blakoe" ring, which opens and shuts like a bracelet. Any ring can be worn around the base of the penis, or it can be used around both the penile base and the scrotal sack together. The ring works by blocking the blood in the penile veins so that it can't return to the body. Of course, we all know that it's the accumulation of blood in the penis, normally as a result of sexual excitement, that causes an erection. Some rings have attachments in the shape of cockscombs, rubber feathers, and such to stimulate the clitoris during regular intercourse. Some women find that the rings temporarily change the texture of the penis—make it rougher and more knotty—and create greater vaginal friction. Another advantage of the ring is that the penis *temporarily* increases in girth. However, don't let your hopes get too swollen—it won't *stay* that way.

A more complicated variation on the single penis ring is the "Seven Gates of Hell," which consists of seven metal rings attached to a leather thong. The rings decrease from fist size to pinky size and are designed to be fitted around the non-erect penis. Upon erection, it's said to produce a sensation that is crazy-making, although some men find it slightly painful as well as psychologically disturbing; thanks to the unfortunate name, it has overtones of the Spanish Inquisition.

The most important thing to remember about

the penis ring is that, like a tourniquet, if it stays on too long, it can do more harm than good.

If you don't want to spend money on a professional ring, a simple rubber band wound several times around the penis is not a bad substitute!

The Yes Bra

You've heard of the no bra. This is the yes bra, and it's one booby trap that can set off an explosive orgasm. It's a wiry corsetlike attachment with two electrodes that fit over the nipples. The cups are conical pilings of wire that fit over each breast like regular bra cups. A vibrator attachment conveniently located at the waist within easy reach makes the whole thing shake, rattle, and roll its owner into ecstasy. Many women claim that they can have an orgasm this way without even touching themselves down below.

Fly United

I really wouldn't recommend buying stock in this one, but there's a gizmo called the vibro Double Dongo ($14.95) that consists of two penises joined at the joint. A woman can use it by inserting one Dongo in her vagina and the other in her anus. It's also nice for two gay male lovers who aren't speaking; they can have sex together with their backs turned.

As the Worm Turns

A combination vibrator and dildo is the "squirmy." These little buggers (if you want to use them for that) are molded rubber penises containing a motor that makes the squirmy . . . well, squirm.

Some squirmies are made to operate on a masturbatory frequency; others have straps so that they can be worn by one partner and inserted into the other. Frankly, although the sensations produced are very pleasurable, when I see one in action outside the vagina I can't help thinking of the Chiquita Banana girl, or worse, those little wind-up dolls they used to sell on the sidewalk. If you don't harbor these associations—or even if you do—you can have fun with squirmies. You can buy a mini model for as little as $14.95 or a superduper for $20. As yet, they don't sell hula hoops to go with them, but wait . . . just wait.

Better Late than Never

The prophets of old thundered when women fashioned "images of men" and used them for pleasure. In biblical times, only upper-class women had dildos, and many were fashioned of gold and silver.

Nowadays you don't have to make do with gold or silver; you can have latex. The biggest dildo on the market is the mule, eighteen inches of solid rubber in either pink or black. Fortunately, this monster isn't hard, because it doesn't need to be. It's full of ridges and has a big set of balls at the base.

Another eighteen-incher is the double dong, for lesbians or gay men, or straight couples who want to get together in an unstraight way.

The deluxe French dildo is eight inches long and has row upon row of tiny rubber thorns guaranteed to soak the rose with dew. For the monogamistically inclined, there's a dildo carved in the shape of a bride, complete with tickly bouquet and ticklier lace veil, all rubberized of course. The "squirt dinger" ejaculates your favorite liquid (warmed, please) from a hand-operated bulb attached to it.

Thrillo Pads

These are logical sex aids that everyone would do well to own. The Magico Stimulator is an oval-shaped piece of rubber with a hole in the middle that slips over the penis and lies flat against the man's crotch. The smooth side fits next to his skin; the prickly side presses against the entire vaginal area and stimulates everything at once—vulva, clitoris, urethra, and all. It's like a hand cupped over the vulva and is just the assist that every woman needs. The Thrillo Pad looks like one of those scalp massagers with prickly rubber points that you use when you shampoo your hair. It costs only three dollars, and I don't know why no one ever thought of such a cute little thing before. It's better than a clitoral attachment on a penis ring because it covers the entire female genital zone in one fell swoop. It's the handy-dandy way to orgasm—and more-gasm.

Ben Who?

Rounding out the repertoire of female devices is the electric Ben-Wah. In the original, nonelectric form, the Ben-Wah is a small pair of fluid-filled balls designed for insertion into the vagina. The first ball is empty; the second one is usually filled with mercury, securely sealed inside. The volatile fluid, sometimes called "quicksilver," forces the second ball to roll back and forth, hitting the first one. Result: a steady, pleasant series of sensations in the vaginal area as a woman walks, dances, or even rides in a car. Invented by the Japanese six hundred years ago, the Ben-Wah can be worn to work unnoticed (by other people) and used to pass idle moments pleasantly, if not ecstatically. The more vigorous the woman's movements, the greater the sensation; running or horseback riding while wearing a Ben-Wah will usually produce orgasm.

The electric Ben-Wah is a round plastic ball containing a small vibrator motor. It's attached by a long wire to a small remote-control battery pack. When the pack is turned on, the unit vibrates.

Home Remedies

You may be shocked to know that you probably already own some of the most inexpensive sex aids available. Just check your drawers (the ones in the kitchen and bathroom, not the bureau) and try some of the following sexperiments for the budget-minded.

Fill a rubber condom with water and put it in the freezer compartment. When it's good and solid, take it out and use it as a hand dildo on your girl. Anything cold is usually a turn-off, but strangely enough, extreme cold can be unbearably exciting.

For another arctic hand-job that will send chills up and down your spine, put a pair of rubber gloves in the freezer.

Condoms can be padded with raw cotton to increase length and width. If things get a little crowded inside the sheath, use a penis ring or rubber band to hold it on.

Feathers and paintbrushes (for pictures, not walls) make the best clitoris and nipple ticklers of all. Camel's hair and sable are the best turn-ons in brushes as in apparel, an exciting thought if your girl is acquisitive.

These ideas should give you a start on thinking up other do-it-yourself (if you can't find anyone else!) sex aids. The price of everything is sky-high these days, but with a little ingenuity, you don't have to spend a bundle to keep the home fires cooking.

If You Can't Be Near the Girl You Crave ...

Buy an artificial vagina. The world's most coop-
erative vagina comes in a variety of models.
There's a small—i.e., life-size—replica of the real
thing, complete with hair, which you hold in your
hand while you thrust into it with your penis.
The larger, "pump" model has a bulb that you
squeeze to simulate vaginal pulsations, and you
can make the pulsations as fast or as slow as you
like. There's also a "foam" model that produces a
nice gooey effect inside, and there's one that
sloshes warm water around your penis. For the
thorough-minded man, there's a "me, too" model
that contains an anus as well as a vagina. Twelve
to sixteen dollars will get you the quietest
girlfriend you've ever had. Not a peep out of
her—just a gurgle of pleasure now and then.

Irresistible, Inflatable You

This is the famous adult-sized rubberized doll
long advertised in magazines as something "to surprise your friends with." The copy goes on to tell
you that you can take her to parties, to the bowl-
ing alley, or ride with her beside you in your car
(as long as you detour past the funny farm).
The key line in the ad is "lifelike in every detail," and you know what *that* means.
You can do everything to her that you've ever

wanted to do to a real, live woman except punch her in the jaw and make her cry. She'll only bounce back.

The Potion That Puts You in Motion

Here's an easy-to-mix aphrodisiac containing staple ingredients that you're certain to have in your kitchen at all times:

Take half a dozen quail eggs, a handful of peanuts, tree bark, sugarcane, alcohol, and ground-up bull testicles. Put them all in the blender, throw the switch, then buy a new blender.

This supposedly potent-making brew is on sale at market stalls in Salvador, Brazil, a city that has the reputation of being in the most passionate area of a passionate country. The natives claim it will make you a better lover than Don Juan—at least, that's what they tell the tourists. Some of the horniest witch doctors I know swear by it on a stack of drums. As for me, I don't know of any surefire aphrodisiacs. It's really the notion that puts you in motion.

Gimmicks and gadgets can be lots of fun, but there's one thing to keep in mind at all times. Don't get attached to your attachments! Don't let them make you too lazy to go out and do the real thing. Most of all, be ever vigilant of the psychological effect they have on you. Learning the art of pleasing another person is one of the wonderful side benefits of sex. Many gadgets and gimmicks are designed solely to please oneself. Overdo it, and you'll find you've entered a strange and lonely world. So have a solo fling or two, if you wish, just for the hell of it—but keep a good mental balance while you're "tying one on."

My advice is to use these gadgets occasionally for a little spice, but always remember that you have one of the most amazing gadgets of all at your disposal—your God-given sexual apparatus. Given the proper care, and provided you know how to use it, it always works.

17. Dr. Strangelove;
or A New Way to Tie One On

The question going the rounds of today's sexual scene is: "How strange is strange?" Obviously, there are degrees of strangeness (other than those earned by abnormal psychiatrists), and you can indulge in some perfectly healthy strangelove without worrying about being carted off in a straitjacket—although that might turn some people on. After all, most of the "isms" in "abnormal" sex behavior have a perfectly normal side, too, and many of them can be traced back to romantic traditions.

For example, one rather tame form of fetishism—the belief that an object is capable of protecting and aiding its owner—was quite the thing in medieval times and was used with clearly sexual implications. Knights riding in tournaments always tied their ladies' scarves to their jousting sticks or wore them on their metal helmets. In modern times, World War I aviators liked to wear a girlfriend's silk stocking under their leather flying helmets.

Another form of fetishism—the displacement of erotic interest and satisfaction to an object—is more contemporary. Every now and then we hear of a hair fetishist who is caught cutting off a girl's hair in a crowded bus. He's arrested for what is, technically, assault. Yet, in nineteenth-century England, the dashing Byronic lover was expected to beg for a lock of his beloved's hair, which he kept in—you guessed it—a locket. The English mock epic poem "The Rape of the Lock," which always causes such hilarity in adolescent classrooms, concerns a lovesick man who steals a lock of a girl's hair when she's not looking.

Another kinky "ism" is transvestism, or the urge to prance around in clothing or articles associated with the opposite sex. Yet high-school girls have always worn boys' letterman sweaters, and unisex is at least a step toward transvestism, even if it stops just shy of the line dividing male and female. The very worst bugaboo in the annals of abnormality is necrophilism, or a desire to copulate with dead bodies. Yet a modification of this appeared in disguised form in Victorian days, of all times. Widows were not permitted to wear jewelry, but they were expected to wear a "mourning brooch," a pin made from strands of the deceased husband's hair.

It would probably cause a sensation if someone were to state that all men have committed incest, yet it's true if you think about it. A baby boy's penis has been in his mother's vagina, along with the rest of him, during the final stages of birth— unless, like Macbeth, he was a cesarean.

But what about sexual practices that appeal to some of the people all of the time, and all of the people some of the time? There are a lot of these. For example . . .

Of Human Bondage

Pleasure in capture and struggle begins the first time a little boy pinions a little girl's arms. If this *doesn't* happen before you graduate from kindergarten, then I'd say you went to a pretty refined kindergarten.

Many people are confused about the difference between bondage and SM, or sadomasochism, and often think they're one and the same. They aren't. Bondage is exactly what it says, and no more: tying up or restraining of one partner by another. Sadomasochism involves blows or other "punishment."

The chief appeal of bondage is its frustration value. In today's hang-loose world, we can do pretty much what we like as long as we do it in (relative) privacy and with consenting adults. But contrary human nature doesn't always like that much freedom; hurdles, barriers, and difficulties add spice to the soup.

Many women who harbor subconscious sexual guilt enjoy bondage because it removes personal responsibility for the pleasure they receive from sex. If they are bound and tied, they can tell themselves, "What's going to happen will happen because I have no control over the situation." Some women thus find that their most intense orgasms occur when they are totally immobilized.

Both men and women occasionally enjoy being tied up during sex; being unable to make the normal pelvic movements creates a congestion or a concentration of sexual feeling that's deliciously maddening. Immobilization makes you more aware of the condition of your sexual parts. You can't go anywhere or do anything—it must be done *to* you—but that's just what makes it such delightfully perverse pleasure.

The Chain Gang

People are complicated, and appearances can be deceptive, but in my experience there are a few signs that *hint* at a preference for bondage in women. When I had my house in New York, I hired a woman who always lay with her arms over her head and her wrists together while she was making love. Her habit came to my attention when a customer complained that she didn't, as he put it, "huggy bear." I was just about to have a motherly little talk with her when we were raided. Since the bail bond is the same for cuddly and uncuddly hookers, I had more to worry about than huggy-bearing on my staff. But then something happened that made everything hang together. The girl slapped a police matron and was put into handcuffs. As she looked down at her manacles, a glow of pleasure came over her face. I realized then that her standard position was her subconscious way of indicating what she really wanted. When we all got out of jail, I appointed her my "bondage girl," and found a sweet, cuddly huggy bear for the complaining customer. Everybody was happy.

That situation was unusual. What are some of

the more common signs of bondage preference in women?

In my personal opinion, wearing an anklet or ankle bracelet is something to consider. At one time, anklets or "slave bracelets" were all the style, yet not every woman wore one. They're passé now, so especially when I see a woman wearing one today, I always wonder if what she really wants is a somewhat heavier chain—like a manacle.

"Slave" jewelry is another hint. One gold bracelet is not unusual, particularly if it's a very good quality one. But a whole armful of cheapies is something else. Collarlike necklaces, as opposed to pendants, are another sign of *maybe*. Any overindulgence in belly chains is something to wonder about; but remember, these are in now, so perhaps a woman with too many is simply trying to be fashionable.

So much for the women who may want to be tied up. How do you spot the ones who want to do the tying? This is harder, but generally I'd look for a slight air of masculinity or, more specifically, starkness in her dress and manner. Nearly every woman has a tailored trenchcoat, but a bona fide Lili Marlene belted mackintosh is more rare. This the real "spy" raincoat, with lots of flaps and round leather buttons. Back in the days when Marlene Dietrich was at her peak of popularity, these coats were everywhere, but they're less popular now. The woman who seems to have a "thing" about them might be your woman if you're in the market for rope burns.

The woman who wears no jewelry at all may be saying, in effect, that *she* intends to remain unshackled. Severity of any kind, whether in clothes or hairdo, is food for thought. A woman wearing a black-leather belted trenchcoat, no jewelry, her hair pulled back in a headache-tight bun may not have the slightest interest in tying *you* up, but we can be pretty damn sure you'd better not try to tie *her* up.

The Rope Grope

Restraining devices can be as simple as the contents of the average kitchen utility drawer or as complicated, authentic, and expensive as a complete full-sized set of town stocks.

However, all you need for a modest dip into bondage are four short pieces of rope and four bedposts. If you have an early-American fourposter bed, it's only fitting and proper that you begin your pursuit of kinky happiness with a spread eagle.

Tying up your woman in this position is a good way for both of you to practice the kind of clitoris-centered missionary position I described in an earlier chapter. Her legs will be flat on the bed, spread but not raised, and you will be on top of her—the better to rub her clitoris, no? If you're a guy who orders "Put 'em up!" bondage is the best way I know of to get out of the habit.

A woman who has a spread-eagled man at her disposal is even luckier. I often tie up my lovers when I'm in the mood to get on top, because I've found that too many men won't lie still and let the woman do the work in this position. They still hump and bump—or try to—and it spoils my concentration on my rhythm. It's hard for the man to thrust *up* proficiently, so when we're on top, we women would rather a man keep entirely still.

The best way to keep him still is to tie him to the bed. For the man who would like to be passive occasionally but can't bring himself to do it for reasons of pride, being restrained provides him with a perfect excuse. His wrists and ankles may be abraded, but not his ego.

Oral sex is *great* under bondage! Too many recipients of fellatio and cunnilingus are their own worst enemies because they get too excited and move around too much. The more delicate sensations of oral lovemaking can best be savored when the body is still. A lot of women who are afraid to perform fellatio on a man because of the danger of choking on too vigorous a thrust can do their best tongue work when this worry—silly as it is—is removed.

All Hung Up and Spaced Out

If you want to invest about fifty dollars in a body harness, you'll learn what it means to be well-hung in a different way. Erection almost always occurs during suspension in air, and when you're hung in a body harness, you get a special feeling of combined vulnerability and sensuality.

The male body harness ends in a penis ring and also has sturdy rings at the waist and shoulders for a successful rigging. There's also an optional anal plug for added stimulation. The entire harness can be worn under the clothing for day-long stimulation and anticipation of good things to come.

The female body harness has a labia-spreader that completely exposes the clitoris and vaginal opening to make things easier for the man underneath. Some models for women also have adjustable rings that squeeze the breasts. The weight of the suspended body tugs on the rings and the labia spreader to provide gentle but exciting pinches throughout your harnessing sessions.

You can also buy the labia spreader alone, or the "half-harness" for men, which consists of a heavy leather belt for the waist and either a penis ring or a male chastity cage. The latter is a penis-shaped wire container that permits the wearer to receive oral sex but prevents him from having intercourse.

To use the complete harnesses, you'll need very strong ceiling beams, or rural privacy and a fine old oak tree. The yellow ribbon is optional.

Traveler's Checks and Double-Checks

Locking chastity belts are available in either metal or leather, some of the latter with studs. You may think that this ancient device defeats the purpose of sex, but it all depends on what kind of sex you want.

If you and your woman are in the mood for anal sex, you can lock up your woman's vagina with a standard chastity belt; if you want to practice breast squeezing with no temptations to change your mind, you can get a double chastity belt that seals off everything below her waist. For women who want to make sure no females will ever come near their man, there's a male chastity device called the "meat tenderizer." It looks like a G-string with an opening for penis and testicles, but it's covered with sharp metal studs that would give even the hottest girl pause and would discourage—to say the least—belly-to-belly friendships.

Riding Hell-for-Leather

The unconscious attraction of leather can be easily explained. It's the skin of animals, so when we wear it, we're hinting that we, too, are animals under the skin.

Leather is commonly associated with fetishes of various kinds (the French know whereof they speak when they call leather *cuir*, which is pronounced "queer"), but the animality associated with leather has its tame side, too.

If you can stand the heat, or if you want to lose some weight, try leather garter belts, panties, vests, undershirts, or even a leather bra. You can keep all of these items on while you make love, because the panties have slits in the crotch, and the bras have nipple openings.

One leather item I personally enjoy is a double sleeve. This is a full-length bondage sleeve designed to keep hands and arms immobile behind the back, with lacing that allows for a snug fit. Women with very responsive nipples find that having the arms pulled tight behind the back exerts a delicious tug on the chest muscles that makes their breasts thrust out and perk up. Pour your woman into one of these and suck on her breasts until she has an orgasm. If she knows this is *all* she's going to get, her mind may instruct her body to "make do" and come the only way she can. It works—and even if it doesn't, failing is certainly fun.

Straitlaced Ladies and Other Bondage Freaks

Victorians had more kinky fun than we give them credit for, except in most cases they didn't know they were having it. The whalebone corset, far from causing women agony, was actually a garment that most of them enjoyed immensely. Much of the literature of the era contains testimonials on the joys of tight lacing. Women claimed they didn't "feel right" without their corsets, just as many of today's women make the same comment about their bras. A lot of Victorian women slept in their corsets, and some even tried to keep them on during childbirth.

Anyone who doubts that there was something sexually weird about the tastes of these strapped-in women need only consider the ideal seventeen-inch waist span of a nineteenth-century woman, the same size proudly sported by Scarlett O'Hara. Any woman who went around laced up that tightly *must* have been constantly aware of her body in the most abnormal way. The bodice of the corset pinched her nipples, and the bottom sliced across her lower belly where it would do the most good. In addition to this day-long caress,

a tight corset gave a woman the light-headed,
breathless feeling that we connect with sexual
pleasure.

A more sane version of the nineteenth-century
corset is available today. It's called a waist cincher
and can be worn with old-fashioned stockings for a
session of nostalgic bondage sex. It laces up the
back and makes the belly protrude in a soft little
bulge that many men find appealing in this day of
pencil-slim boyishly built girls. I doubt if there's a
man alive who hasn't fantasized having sex with a
woman who was wearing nothing but a garter
belt, stockings, and high heels. If you substitute a
lacy waist cincher for an ordinary garter belt, you
can feel wicked with a minimum of wickedness.

The Sensuous Scarf

When any one of the five senses is taken away,
nature sees to it that the remaining senses increase
in power. Blind people have great tactile and
smell sense, and deaf people develop sharp eye-
sight.

Blindfolds and masks can often be valid sex aids
for low-response women. Not seeing your lover
can hot things up, because you are forced to *feel*
him. (Instead of Guess Who, you can play Guess
What.) You can use an ordinary scarf, or you can
buy leather and rubber items, including a
"brank," a medieval headsman's hood that was
sometimes adapted for humiliation purposes in
dungeons.

If you've already won the medieval contest of

tilt-a-guilt, you might be ready for fun and games with blindman's buff. A blindfold can also hot things up for the beginner orgiast, whether the blindfold is on you or someone else. And there are those times when you'd rather *not* know who it was.

Adam and Eve and Pinch-Me-Tight

Most women would like steady breast play throughout intercourse, but this is hard to manage in certain positions. A pair of nipple clamps for this purpose, available at sex-toy stores, will keep a good hold on things, or you can use ordinary clothespins. Some women like to wear earrings on their nipples, not only during sex, but during in-heat "oneplay" sessions alone at home. A terrific turn-on is rubbing a heat-producing unguent on the nipples; Ben-Gay, Musterole, or Heet, all used for backaches and muscle sprains, can produce an ideal pain-pleasure sensation when used on the breasts. (*Don't*, however, use any of them on mucous membranes—and you know what mucous membranes I'm talking about.)

Spanks for the Memory

The sea yields much. One of the best places I've ever had sex was on a beach filled with sharp shells. My bottom was a crisscrossed wreck when we finished, and when I soaked it in the salt sea the stinging sensation I experienced made me hot all over again.

Another of nature's best SM aids is something that's hard to avoid on many beaches—sea nettles or jellyfish. A woman I know (who lucky creature, lives on the New Jersey beach year-round) regularly uses them prior to spanking. She first discovered this technique by accident when she was swimming nude and sat on a jellyfish. The sharp sting shortly turned into a warm, sexy glow, making her yearn to be spanked. She had never indulged in any kind of SM before, but suddenly she wanted it. Her lover complied, and they found that a very mild paddling was enough when combined with the jellyfish sting that was already present.

Lest you are now getting ready to run out and look for a jellyfish, let me say that you needn't take me *that* literally. As the hero of Charles Lamb's "Essay on Roast Pig" discovered, you can have cooked meat without burning down your house. You can simulate the effects of a jellyfish with another kind of nettle—prickly branches that are found on roadsides. A switch made of a cluster of nettles feels the same way, and it's certainly much neater than slinging a soggy jellyfish around the bedroom.

There's another item that combines a good sizzle with a nostalgia trip, if you prefer things that way. Buy a pair of men's suspenders—braces, if you live in England—and tan each other's bottoms with them.

Suppose you love to beat on each other, but love each other too much? Try a pair of "batachas," padded clubs that permit you to take a good swing without risking a limb in a sling.

Many of my readers have told me they fantasize about bondage, SM, and other freaky things, but when the time comes, they can't cut the mustard. Either the urge vanishes or else it's shrouded in embarrassment: they feel too silly to follow through.

My advice is this: *don't force it*, any more than you'd force any other sexual situation. All of us have fantasies that are sometimes best left unrealized, and only you can tell for sure which are which. You might dream of whips, jockey bats, riding crops, and jumping feathers, but like many of the horses on which these items are designed to be used, you might be what is known as "crop shy." This is fine; quite often, the real fun in strangelove is the planning, dreaming, and talking.

If you do make this scene, always be sure that you know your partner well and trust him or her implicitly. Strangelove is a game for friends, not strange bedfellows. Otherwise, it can get rough—much too rough for comfort.

18. The Generation Gap; or Can You Cut It in December as You Did in May?

Old goats and racy mature ladies, unite! You have nothing to lose but your false public images. In fact, you've already lost them. One of the best things about the sexual revolution is that it has corrected the old idea that sex is solely for the young. If you don't believe me, just look around. There was a time in the not-too-distant past when a politician of seventy would have committed professional suicide had he married a very young woman; yet Senator Strom Thurmond of South Carolina has done it and survived. Now he not only kisses babies, he has 'em! The Thurmonds recently became parents of a son.

Older women who took up with young men used to be even more scorned, but now they're looked up to as the smart set—Sybil Burton, Dinah Shore, and Merle Oberon are dazzling examples. Books have been written about them, and the media are full of their pictures and stories. Public television reveled in the life and young lovers of Georges Sand, and—surely a historical first—people are now thinking of Winston Churchill as "Jennie's boy" because the story of his mother's *very* young consorts topped the best-seller lists and overshadowed the extrasexual exploits of her legendary son.

In Praise of Older Women

When I had my house in New York, many of my customers asked me to help them with their premature-ejaculation problems. Few of them could last longer than two minutes, and many couldn't go even that long. All of the men I talked to told me the same story: their sexual timing had been conditioned early in life, usually in their teens, during back-seat quickies in the car with a very young and very frightened girl. As one man put it, "I always had to hurry, hurry, hurry. The girl either had to get home before eleven o'clock, or else she had the weird idea that the longer it lasted the more chance there was of getting knocked up."

These problems could be avoided if more young boys had their first experience with "a woman who knows what she's doing," as the old-fashioned phrase put it.

I've been that woman many times; a lot of fathers have brought their sons to me for sexual initiation, and I still think it's the best way.

In today's free atmosphere, many older women are now admitting what society used to require them to hide—that, like lecherous old men, they get a thrill out of relieving youth of its innocence, or, in other words, "copping a cherry." This is no news to young clergymen of all faiths, who have traditionally been pursued by hot flocks of females on the sometimes naïve assumption that they must be virgins or near-virgins. Now women are free to admit that unsullied youth, or *real* innocence, is even more appealing than the symbolic innocence of the cloth.

Another reason for the older "Mrs. Robinson's" franker interest in young men is her own increased sexual needs. A young man or a teenage boy can "go more times" than a man her own age, giving her quite a run for her honey.

The situation would seem to be ideal for a sexual bonanza across calendar lines. Older women can't stop—and young boys can't wait to begin. Yet there are barriers preventing these two grandly glandularly compatible groups from getting together on an all-out basis.

Getting Man-Child to the Promised Land

There are some pitfalls an older woman should avoid with her teenage lover. If you expect to get your paperboy past rustling his papers to rustling your sheets, here are some things to watch out for.

1. The way to his penis is *not* through his stomach. The question of maternal instinct is so fraught with emotion that we'll never really know whether it actually exists or not, but thanks to this confusion, some women, out of guilt, summon up their maternal instinct at the worst possible times.

I realize that most teenage boys *look* starved all the time. They're tall, skinny, and generally peaked. To make matters worse, their reputation for eating whole refrigerators full of food is firmly

established, so that when older women try to
think of ways to lure them, the first thing that
comes to mind is food. Getting a boy into the
house is no problem; keeping him there is, but
the last way to go about it is to say, "Let me get
you something to eat." The kid is probably feeling
a little uptight at this point, and not at all hungry
—at least, not for food. He'd rather listen to a good
rock record, if you have one, to be followed by
getting his own rocks—and yours—off while the
beat goes on.

2. Never mind what he's studying. The very
worst way to remind a boy of his tender youth is
to ask him what grade he's in, yet many older
women trying for an opener will fall into this
trap. The next-worst ploy is any mention of homework. You'll only date yourself—they don't *have*
homework anymore. At least, none of the kids I've
seduced seem to. So never mind what he's *been*
studying. This is a whole new curriculum.

3. Don't expect to be seduced yourself. This one
is to laugh. It's true that Romeo was only a teenager (and even then it was Juliet who took the initiative), but *we're* dealing with reality. If you're
going to wait for a teenage boy to make the first
move, you may as well get out the checkerboard
and resign yourself to a nice quiet afternoon of
drafts. The most important thing to remember is
that *you* are the adult. Take charge of the situation in a nonaggressive way that still has quiet
overtones of authority. Remember, he's been told
what to do since birth, and he's still in the habit
of being led.

4. Don't expect anything fancy. Youth may be
daring and adventurous in many ways—but not in

bed. The average young boy is not going to pour wine in your navel and lap it up. This sort of lovemaking is the province of experienced, ultrasophisticated men—who have learned from a wised-up woman like you somewhere along the way—but too many older women assume that young boys will automatically behave like the hero in a French novel. Just because a middle-aged husband is too tired or embarrassed to do such things does *not* mean that a young man will do them. What you can expect from a young lover is good hard sex with lots of repeat performances and very little conversation—which is what you want from him, isn't it?

Here is my tried-and-true method for getting it on with a teenage boy—with a view to getting off.

Make the logistics of the situation as easy for him as possible. Meet him at the door in a housecoat with nothing under it, explaining to him that you were napping. Don't try to play the femme fatale and wear your most glamorous dress; glamorous dresses tend to be very complicated and full of hooks, eyes, and difficult buttons. Such obstacle courses are fine for the experienced lover, but your young boy is probably painfully aware of his clumsiness and might not last through the first hook without acute embarrassment over his lack of dexterity.

Be casual about your state of undress, so that your initiate will get the message. Don't pull open your robe and expose yourself like the September morn; instead, sit down, cross your legs, and let your robe fall partially open to the thighs. This "accident" will usually cause a boy's eyes to bug out, even though he tries mightily to look the other way.

This is the moment to murmur something inviting and just a bit bold. Try this: "I don't mind your looking at me. In fact, I find it flattering."

Remember that, while he's probably a virgin, he's not nearly so innocent in every other way. Enough has been written about older women, enough movies have taken up the subject to put the idea in your young virgin's head. (Remember Mrs. Robinson? And Deborah Kerr in *Tea and Sympathy*?) Bank on the fact that he's *heard* plenty about naughty women like you, even though he probably was never near one before.

Once you decide he's ready for actual contact—a quick glance at his crotch will give you the signal—take command of the situation. Maternalism is out, but a slight schoolteacherish touch will help things along; chances are he's had at least one crush on a slightly older teacher, so if you make it clear that he's going to *learn* something from you, he'll feel more at ease.

This is the time for the direct approach. Tell him you're very much attracted to him and ask him if he would like to make love to you. (He'll say yes.) Ask him to help you undress—not that you have far to go—and then help him take off his clothes.

Familiarize him with the various parts of your body, starting with the parts that boys don't usually fantasize about, such as your shoulders and the insides of your thighs. By the time he gets to the real goodies, you won't have to guide him. He'll be in overdrive!

Leave his genitals alone during this stage of the

game. If you fondle him—the jig will be up in jig time. He wants to be a man and get in where a man is supposed to get in. No matter how fierce an erection he may have (and he'll have a real rock!), don't pay any attention to it—yet. Don't even look at it.

Now have him insert one finger into your vagina, explaining as he does so that the creases he feels will stretch out and become smooth during intercourse. Anticipate what he's feeling as he probes you.

When the time comes for him to enter you, *move fast*. Don't—I repeat, don't—bother about getting comfortable, going to a bedroom, pulling down the spread, or getting him completely undressed. If you linger too long over any of these rituals, he'll either lose his erection or ejaculate prematurely. A boy's first encounter with sex is fraught with mental pitfalls. It's vital that he know that he's capable of getting penis into vagina. Once he's cleared that hurdle, he'll be putty in your hands, and you can mold him in any way you wish. His confidence is your ace in the hole, so to speak.

Many older women complain that a young boy doesn't last long enough. Of course he doesn't—not the first time. Expect him to explode inside you within the first few minutes, or even seconds. The satisfying aspect of sex with a boy his age is his repeater capacity. He'll be ready for another round in an unbelievably short time, and you won't have to do a thing except be there. Sometimes, his first erection won't even go away before he's ready for the next round. Many young boys can last through

six or seven rounds with a perpetual half-hard-on!
Ah, youth!

The Torso That's More So

Many older women worry unnecessarily about
the state of their bodies. I know a boy of eighteen
who told me that he sleeps exclusively with
women over thirty because they're cleaner! As he
puts it, "The last girl of my own age I slept with
had a gunky belly button."

Many young men are discovering that the famous quality known as "It" that older women are
said to have is really very easy to define. "It"
means owning more than two pairs of ragged blue
jeans. "It" means wearing perfume, and "passé"
counterrevolutionary things like black-lace nightgowns. No matter how much antiestablishment
young men try to deny it, there's nothing quite
like a glamorous, *feminine* woman in Chanel No.
5 with a well-trained Channel No. 1.

Young men also enjoy the older woman's body.
Being slender has become a cliché; most males,
young or mature, still like a little flesh on their
woman. In other words, these young rascals really
dig a torso that's more so. The unisex look is beginning to get on male nerves.

If you have figure faults, or are simply not
quite what you used to be, there are ways to mini-
mize such things, and fortunately the older
woman has enough common sense and know-how
to do it tactfully. If you don't wear a bikini well,
don't go to the beach with a young lover. Instead,

be the queen of the night with him. Use dim lighting at home, and make sure the light is always behind you when you're full-length and nude. The effect will be electrifying!

More important, don't worry about not being a perfect 34-24-34. In the first place, he'll be too excited and delighted to notice. In the second place, you're doing him the favor of his young life, and he'll be much too grateful to dream of criticizing his lucky conquest, even to himself.

The Nostalgia No-No

It's best to let your young lover do his rapping with a girl his own age. The two of them can sit on the floor all night long and emerge with nary a wrinkle or shadow. Most women over thirty-five should refrain from getting into long conversations with young lovers, because they invariably tend to talk about things that are best left unsaid.

Stay off the subject of Franklin D. Roosevelt or else you'll find yourself reminiscing with: "Remember when he . . ." and before you know it, you'll be doing one of the familiar imitations. Skip old movies and related nostalgia. What seems like only yesterday to you will seem like yesterday's history quiz to your young lover.

The Older Man

Society has always been much more liberal about older men and younger women than about

the opposite situation. In an old New England
graveyard you can find a big tombstone noting the
final resting place of one Hiram Perkins, surrounded by four or five smaller tombstones, all reading
"Beloved wife of." The newest stone, denoting the
whereabouts of the last B.W.O., is carved with
unashamed dates proving that she was all of sixteen when old Hiram married her. I don't need to
tell you who outlived everybody in the plot.

The appeal of older men is made up of many
intriguing factors. One very minor thing, but one
which I've always found charming, is the way hair
grays. Men tend to gray at the temples first, and
this looks distinguished. There's also the money
angle. While it's fun to sit on a bare floor and
drink cheap wine with a young man your own
age, most young women are easily impressed with
luxury. An older man is, as they used to say, "established," and can afford to do the things that
impress her—whether she's willing to admit it in
so many words or not.

This is much more of a factor than the so-called
father-complex attraction, which most psychiatrists
now believe is of minor importance. It's significant
that beautiful young women seldom develop a father complex when it comes to impoverished
older men.

Finally, there's the simple matter of the amount
of time men of different ages spend with a
woman. A man in college has his classes to attend,
one or more part-time jobs, plus the usual number of extracurricular activities. An older man has
paid his dues and has plenty of time for nocturnal
action. In any case, his studying days are behind
him and his job is under control as well as secure.

He's not going to be bushed, because he knows how to pace himself.

Best of all, an older man knows something about sex that younger men usually have yet to learn—how to go down on a woman. Cunnilingus has been called the old man's specialty. This can often be a left-handed compliment, because many people still think: What choice does he have? This isn't true; it's merely that an older man is more interested in pleasing a young woman than he is in pleasing himself. I wasn't a girl when I met the elderly but still quite virile comedian whose penchant for very young girls was as famous as his jokes. His years didn't slow him up in either department—a masterly job of cunnilingus, followed by a lusty lay in the hay. In fact, he was a good example of the "staying power" that mature men have. Forget the jokes about how "it takes them all night to do what they used to do all night." They may be good for only one orgasm of their own—but think of how many the woman can have during that nice long sex session.

I've known older men who could go on for an hour of cunnilingus, with every evidence of intense pleasure. One such man told me that he had actually developed a "deep-throat" condition as he grew older. His pleasure in *giving* had become so highly developed that he actually felt orgasmic sensations in his mouth and tongue. This kind of transference of feeling has often been observed in men who have been wounded in the crotch in wartime. It can also be achieved by hypnosis; genital sensations can be transferred to other nonsexual parts of the body. I've experienced a kind of self-hypnosis in this way. Once, while a lover was playfully sucking my big toe, I invented a fantasy that my toe was actually my penis. I pretended that I was a man and that my lover was a woman going down on me, and for a couple of mad minutes it was actually true!

Breaking the Slanguage Barrier

Slang, of course, dates everybody, and very quickly, too. Some of the cool phrases of the sixties already sound quaint, such as "sit-in," "swim-in," or any other kind of "in."

There are other, nonslang expressions that are just as troublesome but much harder to avoid, because they are—or were—standard good English at one time.

Here's a "watch-out" list for the edification of older women and men who like to have social and other intercourse with members of the opposite sexual and generational persuasion.

Pearl Harborites	Post-Vietnamites
Victrola	stereo
Negro	black
homosexual	gay
stockings	panty hose
rouge	blusher
lipstick	lip gloss
portable radio	transistor
pocketbook	paperback
bathing suit	bikini
charge plate	credit card

I've learned from hard experience the most important rule in dealing with a younger lover: *Don't buy his or her love*—unless your pocketbook and your ego can afford it.

I once became involved with a boy of eighteen. They say pride goes before a fall, and it must be true, because my first thought was, "I can still get a teenager." Our lovemaking was great, but then something happened that made me furious and for which I have no one to blame but myself. I went away for a week and left my lover in my apartment. I told him to order anything he wanted and to help himself to the phone.

He did just that—not surprisingly. I said to, didn't I? *But I really didn't mean it.* Subconsciously, I was testing him, hoping that when I returned he would have zero bills waiting for me, which would have "proved" that he wanted me for myself.

I returned to a four-hundred-dollar bill from the top gourmet grocery in town (they *do* eat a lot at that age) and a two-hundred-and-fifty-dollar phone bill.

I promptly blew up and ripped the phone out of the wall, then dragged all the jars of *foie gras* off the kitchen shelves and smashed them on the floor.

I could easily have afforded the six hundred and fifty dollars, but I didn't want to pay it for reasons of pride. I shouted at him, "I'm the hooker around here, not you!" It wasn't my finest hour, but I learned something from it, so I'm glad it happened.

Yes, youth is wasted on the young. And gold is often wasted on the old. But you can't buy one

with the other. However, you *can* rent it—if that's
what you want—and I have no quarrel with those
who do. I'm speaking only for myself. I think
youth and age have so much to offer each other—
in the way of novelty, sexual and psychological
education, and a damn good time both in and out
of bed—that it's better than an even exchange. It's
more like seventy-thirty—with *both* partners getting the seventy percent!

19. Sexual Etiquette

Bedroom manners (or the lack of them) can make all the difference between good and bad sex—or no sex at all. One of the most popular girls at my New York house was neither pretty nor an especially good lay. (I know; I checked her out!) But she was so considerate, so thoughtful, so tactful toward the other person, that her just-average performance in the sack turned into a "beautiful experience," as one of my customers called it.

Sexual etiquette, along with every other kind, often gets lost in the shuffle today. People say to one another, "Let's fuck," thinking they're being sophisticated and liberated, but I would never permit such an approach in my home—and not even in my house when it was not a home.

As a European, I was raised with a lot of formality, and as a madam I set an example that my customers appreciated and followed. I never referred to my customers as "Johns," for example, nor would I permit my girls to do so. The men appreciated it, and showed their appreciation with gifts. Sometimes the gifts were expensive, often they were nothing but a few flowers or a scarf. Their cost was not important; the feeling behind them was what mattered. The men were saying:

"Thank you for treating me like a human being and not just another customer."

You can't apply the principles of sexual etiquette too early in the game. If you wait until you're actually in bed, chances are it'll be too late. Chances are even better that you'll never get as far as the bed!

Let's check out the "manners that maketh the man" through an entire evening, from the first gleam in the eye all the way through.

Easy Come, Easy Gauche

Corniness and rudeness are hardly the same thing, since the intention is different, but the effect is pretty much the same. What looks like a smooth approach in the late-late movie will only make a fool of you in the seventies. For example, the most dated thing you can do in a bar is to enlist the waitress as your own personal Miles Standish and ask her to tell a woman: "The gentleman at the bar would like to buy you a drink."

This places a woman in an awkward position right off the bat, chiefly because it involves an element of female psychology that escapes most men. If the woman says yes, she's admitting *to another woman* that she's on the prowl.

Worse, it makes you look like a timid soul because you've enlisted a third party as your advance scout. The whole thing is unconfortably triangular all around. Worst of all, if the woman says no, the waitress will be the first to know that you struck out. Now you've embarrassed yourself in front of *two* women.

Something even cornier has to happen if the woman accepts the drink. When it comes, she may feel she has to go through the late-late-movie ritual of raising the glass, smiling a feline and seductive smile over the rim, and take a ceremonial sip as you raise your glass in a little toast. Then she has to lift her glass in a little toast to you. . . . It's corny enough to make you barf, right?

If the woman is sitting at the bar, the wisest thing for you to do is act as your own scout by slipping unobtrusively onto a closer stool. If she's seated at a table, my advice is: *watch it*. A woman alone at a table is saying, in effect, that she wants to stay that way. There's a great psychological distance between the tables and the bar, even in today's freer world. If she's in the mood for jumping into the sack, she'll probably jump up on a stool first.

If a man is gauche, the woman gains nothing by being even more gauche. Many feminists are triggered into a rage if a man sends over a drink, because they think he's implying that he has more money than they do. One such woman answered the waitress with, "He may be at the bar, but he's no gentleman!" in ringing tones that the whole lounge heard. Women should realize that a man lays his ego on the line at times like this. Why hurt him beyond fending off—or ignoring—his advance?

Eye Contact vs. Losing Contact

Basically, a little staring goes a long way. We must indulge in some eye contact, because the eyes are the first indicators of what others think of us. However, a lot of men carry it too far. If you've ever tried to outstare a cat, you know what I mean.

One penetrating gaze is enough. If a woman is interested in you, she'll return it, then drop her eyes quickly. Keep watching her (without staring); if she raises her eyes in your direction again, it's a green light.

Do *not* get carried away and go into one of those Valentino-doing-the-tango glazes. I witnessed one of these performances in a New York bar where a man was staring his eyes out at a woman. His eyes opened wider and wider, when suddenly his contact lenses fell out and he panicked, shouting, "Don't anybody move!" Several women screamed, thinking it was a holdup.

Jerks and Other Boudoir Blunderers

Every woman can add an item or five to the long list of examples of bedroom rudeness. Some guys will simply never learn that "lewd" and "crude" are different words. Admittedly, it's difficult for any man to make his way through the mine field of the female psyche without triggering an explosion once in a while.

Women can be dreadfully rude, too, and I'll get to that subject presently. But the female of the species has the edge on manners, because little girls are taught to be tactful as soon as they're old enough to understand. Little boys are allowed to develop along more natural lines, so by the time they become big boys, things can get so natural it's enough to turn your stomach.

Such as . . .

The toilet seat. Next to losing her virginity to a brontosaurus, a woman's greatest shock comes when she sits on a toilet seat that's not there. If she's petite, she can actually fall in and get splashed. It's happened to many women. *Please*, gentlemen, remember to put it back down when you finish!

"How many lovers have you had?" This is the most tactless question a man can ask. It's a typical new lover's error; if he doesn't ask it the first time you sleep together, chances are he won't ever. He usually saves it for that moment that is poetically referred to as the "afterglow." An inquisitive lover can turn it into a third degree.

How can a girl handle this cross-examination?

1. Stony silence. This might be unwise, because he might think you're counting. Since he's already proved his obtuseness by asking the question in the first place, he'll probably be obtuse enough to think that you simply didn't hear him and ask it again.

2. Anger. You're technically correct to tell him it's none of his business, but this response implies you've had scores of lovers.

3. The smokescreen. It takes a special sort of woman to pull this off, one with a gift for maintaining a flow of conversation about nothing at all. If your new man asks his tactless question, roll forward, brakeless, downhill, with something like this: "Pass me the ashtray, please. I bought it at Tiffany's. Foolish, I know, to spend so much on an ashtray, but I believe in buying good things. See how heavy it is? I just love weighty things, don't you? Once I bought a cheap copper-colored lamp, and ..." get the idea?

4. Pure-brass nerve. Depending on your age, you can simply tell every man he's the second. He'll *know* he's not the first, but he just might believe he's number two in the slot. You can use this up to age twenty; after that, you'd better tell him he's the *third*. After thirty, you're on your own.

5. The smooth approach. Sigh and say, "It doesn't matter, they weren't important. You're the one who counts." This answer contains the sly sort of flattery that men gobble up. (It also proves you're much more polite than he is.) Don't worry; he won't catch on to the double meaning about being the one who is doing all the counting, or trying to.

6. Unforgettable you. Answer a question with a question that will rock him on his butt: "Do you just want to know how many *men* I've slept with, dear, or the grand total?"

What to Do with Your Old Rubbers

Most men nowadays assume a woman is on the pill. A lot of men would like to assume it but can't quite bring themselves up to that level of trust with someone they've just met. So they blurt out, "Are you on the pill?" Frequently, the tone of voice has a hint of suspicion in it: "Even if you say yes, how do I know you're not lying to me?"

Most women are not offended by the curiosity; after all, he has a right to know the possible results of his actions. But when the tone of the question is offensive, a woman has a perfect right to say any of the following:

1. "No, I use a hemlock leaf as a sperm catcher. It's an old Mohawk contraceptive."

2. "I'm sterile. Gonorrhea does that, you know."

3. "Don't worry about a thing, I'm already pregnant."

If you're an expert at keeping a poker face, you could try this ploy: "The pill? What do you mean? Vitamins?"

Usually a woman will give a man a straight answer—yes, she's on the pill, and sometimes her reward will be to hear: "Well, I guess I'd better use a rubber anyway." This is tantamount to saying that she probably has the clap, so he'd better be on the safe side—which is precisely what he means.

If you're worried about catching VD from a new girlfriend, use a condom, but don't insult her. Say instead, "I can last longer for you if I use something."

It's not necessary to call a condom anything. She knows what they are. Most of the nicknames for them are unromantic anyway, particularly those two charmers "raincoat" and "safety."

When the time comes to dispose of it, please don't tie a knot in it and toss it on the nighttable or in the bedroom wastebasket. Or even in the bathroom trashcan. Flush it down the toilet, and do it promptly. Above all, don't test it by running water in it and holding it up to reassure her. If you want to play around with balloons, go back to kindergarten.

The Spy That Came in from the Medicine Cabinet

A man who has been around the house for a while will naturally share, to a modest extent, the medicine cabinet in a woman's apartment. A new lover who pokes around here is a natural-born snoop, in addition to being a rat. If he hasn't begun keeping his own possessions in your medicine cabinet yet, this reconnaissance can only bode ill. It has to mean one of four things. He's looking for another man's shaving equipment, which means he's jealous. Or he's a hypochondriac and wants to see what diseases you have that you could give him. He's hooked on something and wants to see if he can borrow some from you. Or he might simply be a pharmaceutical nut who likes to look at other people's array of medicine bottles.

A new lover who spends the night at a woman's apartments naturally needs to use certain things like mouthwash, but a well-bred man will automatically ask permission. And he will pick up the mouthwash bottle without fishing around the entire cabinet first. Remember that sexual intimacy doesn't give the right to *every* other kind.

To encourage a new man on the paths of sexual etiquette, keep some paper cups handy. We know *you* swig directly out of the Lavoris bottle, but does he need to know?

My special twitch in this matter is *over* politeness. If he wants to *use* your mouthwash, okay. But when he asks, "May I *borrow* some mouthwash?" I ask you, how in the name of God can you return a mouthful of mouthwash?

Why Can't a Woman Be More like a Man?

Most female offenses against sexual etiquette are caused by the sheer complications of being female. In order to be fastidious, a woman must paradoxically run the risk of being offensive. Some of the things women do that turn men off are:

Strewing things. The best way to get at beauty aids in a hurry is to leave them lying around in the bathroom. Foremost of these is the dirty powder puff. Men don't understand that you have to *break in* a powder puff the way a man breaks in a new pipe. Other favorites are the uncapped lipstick, the gooey mascara brush, and the hairbrush with great puffs of snarled hair sprouting out of it. If you want to give him a start, however, leave your artificial eyelashes on the washbasin neatly positioned to look like a pair of empty eyes staring up at him.

Even the most sophisticated man is a little taken aback by the sight of those blue boxes on the floor behind the toilet—which he *always* sees because he has to face that way while he pees. To you they're Tampax but to him they're something he'd rather not contemplate. The same cautionary principle holds true about hanging your douche bag on the back of the door. To you it's a douche bag; to him it's an enema bag. Either way, put it away.

What you should hide, in addition to the foregoing, are skin medications, laxatives, corn pads, depilatories (any kind of "tories" are depressing), anything labeled "for the relief of," and all prescriptions that threaten ten years in prison for attempting to refill them without another prescription. There are only a few items a man *should* see. Expensive perfumes head the list.

In other words, men are incurable romantics (the lovable slobs).

Killing with Kindness

Women are warned so much about being tactful that it can backfire. The road to tactlessness is paved with good intentions, and women have been known to pull some beauts in the name of kindness.

To soothe the impotent man: "That's all right, it doesn't matter, I don't care."

To soothe the man who can't make her come: "That's all right, it doesn't matter, go ahead."

To soothe the man who just came in her and now wants to follow up with some oral sex: "Wait! Let me wash first, I'm dirty!"

To soothe the small man who's just apologized for being small: "It's big."

To soothe the big man who's just apologized for being big: "It's not all *that* big."

Sexual etiquette is basically a very simple matter if you remember that etiquette—like sex—is essentially a giving and a getting. You ask politely for what you want, and after you've had it, you remember to say thanks. And not just with words, but with an affirmative attitude and manner that lets your partner share in your glow of appreciation.

20. Oneplay; or Autoerotic Doesn't Mean Loving Your Car

In previous chapters we talked about foreplay. We also talked about fiveplay, sixplay, and sevenplay. This chapter is about oneplay, and I've left it for the last because, after all has been said and done, there are moments when you have only yourself—and why not learn how to be your own lover? That's the first and most important step in learning how to love someone else. An ability to accept your body and its feelings totally, every day and everywhere, is the vital key not only in sexual success but also to supersexual success, and that's what this book is about. It's the single basic point behind all that I've discussed in these lessons in love. Unless "oneplay" is part of your sexual repertoire, you can't play happily with anyone else.

By "oneplay" I don't mean masturbation, although that's an ingredient, and a priceless one at that. Oneplay is the art of being *self*-conscious as opposed to being self-*conscious*. It might be called creative self-love. If it's true that we must learn to love ourselves before we can learn to love others—and I certainly believe that—then it must be equally true that we must learn how to arouse ourselves sensually before we can do the same for others.

Generally, oneplay can be practiced all day, every day, because it's not an outward act so much as an inner feeling. It's being your body's best friend instead of its worst enemy.

Big Kicks from Tiny Tricks

You can live in a perpetual aura of sensuality if only you'll let yourself. As the whole world knows from my previous books, I can even come close to having an orgasm in my ear! I explained in *Xaviera on the Best Part of a Man* that when I wiggle my little finger in my ear to stop an itch, I experience a popping feeling and an intense relief that is definitely sexual.

From an acceptance of little "sensualities" like this come the greater pleasures of bedding down. The trouble is, not many people arrive at adulthood without a warped attitude toward sensual acceptance. Even the most uptight people know the furtive pleasure in scratching off a scab or peeling a sunburn. They're enough into oneplay to react to these things, but they're furtive about it because, as children, they were told, "Stop fooling with yourself!" Many enlightened parents, who accept masturbation in their children and are progressive about their sexual education, persist in nagging their kids about the little things that make up self-exploration. Such parents undermine their constructive attitude about the genital area by their negative attitude about all the other pleasurable areas, making their children the enemies of their own bodies.

Of course, there are certain minor operations that you shouldn't perform on yourself when other people are around. But there are many non-sexual sexual pleasures you can enjoy that will train you, so to speak, to enjoy the sexual ones when you *are* around other people—or one special person.

I love to get sand in my hair at the beach and pick it out later. The grainy feeling on my scalp is oddly enjoyable. I don't know why, and I don't care, because I'm into oneplay.

Smelling your sun-warmed skin is another. I often sit with my nose buried in my forearm while reading, after I've been out swimming. The burny smell is like autumn and makes me strangely happy.

I know a woman who has very thick eyebrows and bends the hairs in half and then rubs her finger back and forth over the crease. Instead of delving into psych books to find out if she's a closet lesbian with an urge to rumple another woman's pubic hair, she simply enjoys her idosyncrasy. She says it gives her a "crinkly pleasure." She can't explain what that means, but again, it isn't important to define these things. Just do them if you enjoy them!

A great many women have a habit of taking a strand of hair and twisting it into a tight coil like a pig's tail. "Anal erotic substitution" or some such technical designation? Perhaps, considering the number of women who want to but are afraid to try anal intercourse. But at least they can enjoy something symbolic of the real thing.

So whatever you were taught not to do in childhood, don't be a fool. Start fooling with yourself!

Oneplay from Nine to Five

It's long been a puritan article of belief that sex is the enemy of work. For this reason, we have old adages such as "Never dip your pen in the company's ink" and rules in some companies that employees who "fraternize" will be fired. But there's no office rulebook that says you can't fraternize with your own body.

You can practice oneplay at work with no danger of being found out, if you use a few commonsense precautions. You don't have to run into the john to masturbate. Merely leaning against a warm, turned-on electric typewriter will bring on a burst of sexual self-awareness. Of course, you don't get up, walk around your desk, and lean your crotch into the typewriter. There are curious eyes everywhere, you know. You don't even have to position your crotch anywhere near it.

Since I've turned writer, I've discovered something wonderful about my new profession. Leaning over to erase (which I sometimes do whether I make a mistake or not) does things to my breasts that's quite special. The warmth, plus the buzzy vibration, travels through my nipples and up under my armpits. I've had everything possible stuck in the latter, too, but nothing feels like that buzz.

The office first-aid kit can be a source of

pleasure, too. Sneak some adhesive tape or a couple of Band-Aids and put them on your nipples. As you become excited and your nipples wrinkle up, the little tug is just uncomfortable enough to make you even more aware of your best points. Men with responsive nipples can do this, too.

Advanced oneplayers, or people with unusually strong powers of concentration, can have even more fun at work. A woman I know wears her dildo all day long, holding it in place with a pair of tight rubber bikinis. The heat generated by this material makes things even better, and she can bring herself off merely by walking to the water cooler.

And Making a Night of It

If you think pretty nightgowns are too square for sex, why not enjoy them when you're alone? Wearing a long black-lace gown when there's no one to see it but you does wonders for your sensuality quotient. If you accustom yourself to such treats from yourself, you'll naturally come to expect the best from others with whom you have sex. If you're anything like me, I can guarantee you that it's impossible not to get hot while wearing a sexy nightgown. When you become horny enough to masturbate—don't. At least, not yet. Ordinary masturbation while you're all alone and looking beautiful can be depressing. You feel wasted, and eventually you get irritable as you think: should such a gorgeous creature have to sleep alone?

Instead, appreciate yourself by pretending that you're your own lover, a man, doing the things to you that you normally expect a lover to do. For example, you can practice kissing and sucking your own nipples. Don't remove the nightgown and get into bed; that's too much like plain old everyday masturbation for this special occasion. Scoop your breasts up and out of the front of the gown and blow on your nipples until they harden. Duck your head and dart your tongue quickly, from one to the other, seeing how long you can keep this up without actually masturbating. Then lift your breasts up and try fluttering your lashes over your stiff nipples, vowing not to masturbate until you succeed.

At last, when you have yourself thoroughly aroused and appreciated, you can let go!

Beyond Orgasm

Nearly everyone has a vibrator, and nearly everyone uses it for the one purpose that the ads never mention. Why not do some of the things the ads recommend, such as touching it to your "stiff" neck, your temples, ribs, or even the soles of your feet. Being tickled in any sensitive area is a form of orgasm, you know, because it's a spasm of sorts. I enjoy using my vibrator on the insides of my wrists, the bend of my elbows, and the backs of my knees. Train your instep to be a sexual area by using vibrating stimulation on it. Any part of your body can be "overextended" and trained to do double duty, so to speak, by becoming an erogenous zone. I can even enjoy the feel of my electric toothbrush inside my mouth!

The Job Can Also Be Done by Hand

Philip Roth rocked the country when he described some of Alex Portnoy's creative oneplay techniques. Actually, Alex wasn't all that inventive, but he did have a special flair. Other boys probably use raw liver, but they don't use *kosher* liver, behind a billboard, on their way to a bar mitzvah lesson. Neither do they let their mothers cook it afterward.

Most schoolgirls do a lot of sitting on beds in crowded dormitory rooms. About the only way to sit comfortably on a bed is to tuck one leg under yourself; as a result, many girls have discovered this particular way of masturbating. Stick the ball of your heel where it will do the most good, and wiggle away. Just don't get too down at the heel, that's all.

But this lesson in oneplay is not a lesson in masturbation. In fact, this is Xaviera urging you *not* to concentrate exclusively on your genital areas— or on your partner's. Such concentration means you're not using eighty percent of your body. What a waste!

Supersex can be achieved only by those who train their nerve endings in nonsexual areas, as well as in the genital areas, to respond to sensual stimulus. Once you achieve that, your *entire* body will automatically become aroused every time you make love. And *that's* what I call *supersex*. Why settle for less?